Dark Psychology:

Done-for-You Techniques, Tips, and Methods of Dark Psychology Manipulation

acknowledge that the author is not engaging in the rendering of legal, financial, medical or professional advice. The content within this book has been derived from various sources. Please consult a licensed professional before attempting any techniques outlined in this book.

By reading this document, the reader agrees that under no circumstances is the author responsible for any losses, direct or indirect, which are incurred as a result of the use of information contained within this document, including, but not limited to, — errors, omissions, or inaccuracies.

Table of Contents

Introduction 1

Chapter 1: Day to Day Examples of Dark Psychology 6

The Secret Techniques of the Best Attorneys 8

The Secret Techniques of the Best Salespeople...16

The Secret Techniques of the Best Leaders 24

The Secret Techniques of the Best Public Speakers 32

Chapter 2: Dark Psychology 101 - The Principles of Dark Psychology: 41

Benign/Covert 43

Dark persuasion 51

Mind games 59

Brainwashing 66

Chapter 3: The Dark Triad 74

What is the dark triad? 74

Machiavellianism.....................................76

Narcissism... 80

Psychopaths... 86

Chapter 4: How to read & manipulate people...93

Reading People 93

Understanding the face:........................... 98
Final tips 101

How to manipulate people 103

Chapter 5: Dark Seduction................... 114

Seducing men 114

How to seduce women 122

Chapter 6: Hypnosis and NLP 132
What is hypnosis? 132
Who is most likely to use it on you? 132

Tactics 133

Chapter 7: Case Studies 150

Psychopathy... 152
Ted Bundy 152

Narcissist... 155
Kanye West 155

Machiavellian 158
Mao Zedong 158

Conclusion 161

Bibliography...................................... 167

Introduction

Psychology is the scientific study of the human mind and how it works. Dark psychology focuses on the darker aspects of the human mind and how they can develop into predatory behaviors and/or people, plus the methods they use when these personality traits are prevalent. A good example of this is understanding the nature of people with personality disorders that derail the lives of those with these conditions or the people around them. Knowing how these conditions and why they work the way they do is one of the cornerstones of dark psychology. Another example would be studying the universality of these traits and the circumstances under which they thrive. Although everyone occasionally thinks of committing some heinous act for various reasons, they usually refrain from acting on them. Why then would there be a necessity for dark psychology if the people likely to act on these impulses are so few?

There are several good reasons for one to learn about dark psychology. It may not seem like a big deal, but it may behove you to consider getting clued up on dark psychology after realizing how prevalent it is in everyday life. This may show how necessary the acquisition of knowledge is for you to decide for yourself if you will play the role of the victimizer, victim, or neither. One reason to learn dark psychology would be because of the fact that its use takes place around you every day. You may want to know when it happens so you know if it's necessary to defend yourself or the ones you love from the potentially devastating effects of the uses of dark psychology on unsuspecting victims. Another good reason to learn it may be because you may secretly be making use of some of these methods and tools without realizing it. Learning consciously to harness these tools properly and with caution may improve your life and perhaps even the lives of those around you. If knowledge is power, then dark psychology is definitely one you will want to consider adding to your existing arsenal of powers, be it for defensive or offensive purposes.

Knowing about something that can be used against you gives you agency in those moments when wielding said knowledge can make or break your life. Much like history, your life is probably full of moments where having some insight into dark psychology could have dramatically changed the complexion of your life. Imagine, for example, that you were being bullied and developed some crippling anxiety because of it. Knowing what makes some people predatory in that way and the methods they are most likely to use against you may have given you a nonviolent way of dispatching those who may have victimized you or even prevented it from occurring altogether. Perhaps you found yourself in a situation where someone you had feelings for did not return those same feelings towards you and you still carry the melancholy imaginings of what you could have done had you possessed the proper tools to make the object of your desire yours to have. Do you think your life's story would contain one or more compelling chapters from such times of romantic infatuations blossoming beyond the "admiring from a distance" phase? There are several examples that show the many ways dark psychology can be used by you or on you.

It happens all around you every day. Every moment of every day, there is someone using the techniques, that were developed from studying some of history's most infamous minds, on you. You might, for example, find that there is an employer who uses these techniques on you and your coworkers to accept unfair terms or work conditions. Would it not be in your best interest to know these techniques so you could live your life more on your terms? Or what if you constantly fall for the countless manipulations of sly salespeople who seem impossible to resist? Surely knowing how to negotiate deals that do not end with you getting the short end of the stick could save you the agony of buyer's remorse, so that you could be in charge of your spending, as opposed to some charming sales rep. Would you not like to have your choices truly be your own instead of falling for the tactics of the many members of society who would daily seek to mislead and/or take advantage of our ignorance?

Picking up this book will be the beginning of a new world you never knew existed. Learning about dark psychology and some of the tactics that have been born from studying some of the evilest people in history can show you a side of yourself, and maybe, other people, you may not have known existed so that you can take charge of situations where persuasion or some form of manipulation will be what wins the day. You will learn, for instance, the different tactics that people might use on you every day, sometimes even in your own home. Those we hold dear are often more likely to be the ones who use and manipulate us most often. You will also learn the dark motivations some of these people might have for using these insidious methods on us. Regardless of whether it benefits you or them, it would not hurt to know the kinds of people who would use these kinds of things and why. You may not realize how much you needed this book until you finish reading this book.

Just know that once the knowledge within this book is made known to you, there will be no going back. Your life and interactions with the people around you will take on a different nature as you navigate your life with the knowledge of the dark side of every person and how that might impact you. Whether you use this knowledge for good or evil is completely up to you.

Chapter 1: Day to Day Examples of Dark Psychology

Most people assume that they understand the darker aspects of human nature. They imagine they would be able to see manipulators if they met them and know exactly what to do to keep themselves from being taken advantage of. Most people are wrong.

Evil will not wear a mask that makes it easy to identify. In fact, it will do quite the opposite. It will blend in and gain the target's trust before turning on them and victimizing them. The victim will often realize what's going on when it is already too late for them to do anything about it.

The devil himself is known for taking the ideal form or even appearing as an angel of light. Users of dark psychology are no different. They are master shapeshifters that will take whatever form is necessary to snare their prey. Disguise and deception come naturally to them. So what does one do then?

The best place to start is by educating yourself on their methods. One does not have to use any of them, but they do have to learn enough so they can at least identify the threat when it is present. That is the first step to solving any problem.

The first thing most people don't realize is those dark personality traits are a part of all of us. As such, we all use them to some degree in our daily lives. People around us may even use them on us in ways that are not harmful to us, not realizing what they are doing. Sometimes they may even use them for our own good. Think of mothers telling their kids false facts to get them to eat their vegetables, or trying to trick a drug addicted loved one to go to a place where they'll find their loved ones waiting to ambush them with an intervention.

Well, this chapter will give you some of the examples that you are most likely to meet throughout your life and highlight many of the tricks they might use on you. It leaves out a lot of the more benign examples of the tricks of dark psychology and tells you of the times when there may be high stakes and you cannot afford to be manipulated or blindsided. These can be moments where someone tries to get you to spend more money than you had intended to, or act in a way that may set you down a path that could be disastrous for you.

The Secret Techniques of the Best Attorneys

They have strong opening cases

A strong opening argument can often be the deciding factor when it comes to winning and losing cases or even closing deals with potential clients. It becomes a game of controlling perspectives and the way an attorney opens before jurors, judges, and/or potential clients can be the crucial moment that determines how the rest of their interactions go.

This is a very important thing to remember when trying to persuade like, or prevent being persuaded by an expert attorney. Learning how to take in opening statements, or maybe learning how to give them, can be beneficial when trying to establish a dominant position a persuasive exchange, because that will be the northern star for the rest of the exchange, so remember to open strong and set a firm foundation to build the rest of your persuasion game.

They anticipate the most likely objections

The best attorney knows their own arguments and standpoints so well that they even know the most likely stances people might take against them and prepare to react to those accordingly in advance.

They leave no stone unturned until they are confident that anyone they interact with will leave that exchange feeling like every objection was tended to, and every question answered.

This can be a fantastic tactic to know how to use when you want to set yourself as an authority in any situation and need to push a certain way of looking at things. Learn to anticipate potential arguments and you will find yourself being harder and harder to refuse when trying to persuade someone.

They use storytelling

Being able to tie stories into logical facts is a brilliant tactic attorneys use because the brain is more likely to enjoy listening to a story and absorb the point being made, more than it will when being inundated with a barrage of facts and statistics.

Stories will often bypass the logical part of the brain and make one think more with their emotions than facts will and this is what you want when trying to establish a strong case for yourself.

Just be careful of someone trying to use this tactic against you and making you fall for a bad argument due to them drawing your logical mind into the nearly hypnotized state that comes with being absorbed by a good story. It increases your suggestibility and reduces your ability to focus on the facts.

They know their audience

Great attorneys make it a point to do background checks on the potential jurors and judges they may have to deal with and try their hardest to make sure they can control who is selected to sit in on their cases. If they can control that element, they try to make their arguments, cases, and general way of communicating suit the audience they will be presenting to.

You never know when you might find yourself in a situation when you have to communicate effectively with people who are not used to your usual style. It is imperative that you know as much as you can about the people you speak to if you are to sway them to come over to your side. You want to learn to communicate with them on their level and avoid the risk of not getting what you want due to minor miscommunications and misunderstandings.

They show and not tell where possible

The mind is more drawn in by stories and pictures than it is by pure facts alone. They are often more interesting and easier for the brain to absorb than dates, studies, and statistics. The best attorneys know this better than anyone and use it to their full advantage. They will present evidence where possible, instead of simply referring to it. They will keep referring back to it, even though the audience knows it's there, to keep reinforcing the 'truthfulness' of their cases and re-establishing themselves as the authority in that specific encounter as they have visual evidence of irrefutable truth.

Be aware of someone who constantly harping on about a piece of evidence they may have shown you. Question it despite seeing it. Make sure that you are not falling for the old trick of misdirection just to be misled by a nefarious manipulator.

They are reasonable

There are moments when digging in your heels and locking your jaw can play against you even when you are in the right. Great attorneys know this and can recalibrate themselves to suit the interaction and better increase the chances of them getting what they want.

You can consider doing this in your own life where you find small points where you agree with your opponent to lower their defenses. Once their guard is down, you can go back and show them the logic in your own point of view.

This can be a great tactic since people are more likely to dig their heels in when it seems force is the only way out, so suddenly changing the game on them can confuse them into thinking they are getting what they want (to be understood by others) while you are secretly just ensnaring them in your trap from a different angle.

They appeal to emotion

There is nothing stronger than being able to use emotions to keep someone off balance and have them eating out of the palm of your hand.

Attorneys will often do this by making witnesses angry on the stand to make them slip up in their testimony, if it suits them; making a jury feel bad for a defendant whether or not they are guilty; making potential clients trust them, whether it's in the best interest of the client or not.

Make sure to always keep your head and use your opponent's emotions against them where possible. Winning or losing at games of manipulations often comes down to emotions more than they do with facts. Whether you are trying to convince or prevent yourself from being convinced, keeping your emotions in check while making sure your target does not will be the deciding factor in you walking away as the victim or victor in these kinds of insidious games.

They watch the audience's body language

Body language is often a huge deciding factor in how people see you and how they communicate as well. You will often see the best attorneys change their swagger according to the situation so that their message is being communicated on multiple levels. Moreover, body language taps into people's' mirror neurons and can have their instinct to imitate be used against them.

Mirroring someone's body language can make them feel accepted or slightly intimidated, as if you are reading their minds. Seeing someone mirroring you is often a sign that they are more likely to believe what you are saying. At other times, you want to use this to see how people feel about you and react accordingly where necessary.

Body language skills can be a tool for reading minds and controlling emotions.

They use leading questions

Leading questions is the favorite technique of many people in the legal business because it allows them to control perspectives, which can win or lose cases and future clients.

If someone asks you, "how much do you hate hockey?" They are not giving you the option of liking hockey. The question already assumes you agree with the person asking it and simply demands the degree to which you agree to show that you are on their side.

Be careful of people using questions like this against you. This tactic can have you not realizing that you are being lured into the trap of accepting a premise that is not true to you.

Persuasion is not about right or wrong, it's about winning.

They make sure to stay the course of their arguments

You won't often see expert attorneys getting side-tracked trying to defend non-arguments or even their own dignity unless the case depends on it. The best of them will always make it a point to stay the course of their argument while trying to trip up their opposition with the details of their own arguments.

This is a crucial lesson to learn if you want to be more convincing in your own life. You want to be able to make your own statements and arguments seems stable and concrete while subtly destabilizing that of your opponent. You want them abandoning their game to play yours. Once you have them playing your game, you have secured victory. All you need to do is keep them in your world.

The Secret Techniques of the Best Salespeople

Taking the advisor role

The best salespeople never come across as though they are trying to sell you something right out the gate. They approach as though they are your advisor, guiding you to finding the best product for you.

This is the best way to avoid putting your customer or client on edge and increasing the chances they will buy something. Look carefully at the approach of the next person who tries to sell you something and note how they use this technique to try to put you at ease and make you more suggestible.

Listening skills

The best salespeople know how to listen closely for the smallest detail that might help them close the deal. It might be a sign of hesitation, confidence anything that tells them if you are a target they should be spending their time on and how they should know if it is time to move on.

Usually, we end up being the ones to give these sales people all the information they need to handle us better. All they usually have to do is listen as we over-answer simple questions and give ourselves away.

Empathy

A salesperson who can get under the skin of a prospective client is often more likely to have higher sales because they are able to build a far better rapport with the people they interact with and make them feel safe and secure.

Consider this technique the next time you encounter a salesperson you considered particularly likable. They may just have been using a sense of empathy to comfort you into buying something you may not have wanted in the first place.

Assuming the sale

Salespeople these days no longer ask you if you want to buy their product or not. More often than not they will ask for your details and ask you to sign on the dotted line as if you already agreed to make the purchase.

This often tricks a lot of people into buying things since they don't realize they are being baited into buying something until they're already signing. This tactic is also useful because it takes the choice away from the buyer and puts it in the salesperson's hands.

Confidence

People are a lot more likely to buy with their feelings than with their heads, so a confident salesperson can be highly effective because people are more likely to want to trust them simply because of their confident demeanor.

It's natural to want to follow the lead of someone when they seem like they know exactly where they are going. Salespeople use this information to the fullest by starting the sale with a confident body language that engages you even before any words have been spoken.

Creating a scarcity mindset

The best salespeople know that scarcity and novelty often play a huge role in how we put a value on things. They use this information to make their product seem more valuable by making customers think that this is the best deal they will ever get. They further reinforce this by making customers think that the offer will only stand for a limited time because this is the last one, or another customer showed interest in buying it as well.

Always take your time to know when this pressure is being applied to you or how you could apply it on an unsuspecting victim.

Honesty (where possible)

One of many tactics salespeople have in common with attorneys is their ability to manipulate the truth. They know how to omit certain truths or simply bend the truth where possible to ensure you see the picture the way they want you to.

They will tell the truth where possible and avoid it where necessary. As long as it benefits them, they will play with the truth as much as possible while maintaining a sense of plausible deniability. This way they can practice deception without lying. They escape on a technicality.

Curiosity

Great salespeople will often use questions that seem simple to get what they want from you. They may disguise these questions as simple curiosity, but they are usually laying the groundwork properly to manipulate you into buying what they want.

In the game of persuasion, information is king. The more you know about a target, the more ammunition you have to bypass their rational mind and appeal to their emotions. No word must be wasted and all information must be treasured.

Adaptability

The best salespeople you ever come across will often behave like chameleons. They will observe you and switch whatever details about themselves they need to in order to get under your skin and pull you in. They mold their sales pitch around you.

Getting you to feel comfortable enough to listen and give them more and more of your time is a classic sales technique that ensures that nothing as small as beliefs, moods and/or ideologies impede getting what they want, your money.

Communication skills

It is imperative that a salesperson has the gift of the gab and is quick on their feet because the customers will spend more time listening to the way a salesperson speaks more than they do the actual content of their speech.

Therefore, you will often find that the best salespeople will make subtle changes to the way they use language to better appeal to whoever is in front of them at that moment.

Escalating

Escalation is a great tactic that slowly gets you from the sales floor to the office where the papers await your signature. It involves slowly filling your hands with things or carefully orchestrating the tour so that you finally end up at the office, isolated and comfortable.

This also works well after the sale when one might call you and follow up or maybe even try to get new leads through you. Slowly escalating sets the customer at ease enough to not notice that things are not moving at the pace they intended.

Preparation for objections

As with anything in life, preparation is key. Preparing for possible objections is common among the best attorneys and salespeople. This is a great way to establish and reinforce your position as the expert who needs to be trusted in this given field.

Salespeople take care to make sure they give you the sense that they know more than you and once that has entered your mind, it becomes of the utmost import that they maintain that guise by having all the answers to your questions.

Patience

Patience is a commonly used sales tactic that is seldom recognized by prospective clients. Selling is a process, not an action. The best salespeople will delay you to the point where it becomes a war of attrition.

You could easily be stuck in a salesperson's office for several minutes at a time as they go around finalizing this and verifying that. Do not fall for this trick. It is only to wear down your patience and have you willing to do almost anything to feel the relief of seeing things moving forward, wherever that might lead.

Passion

A passionate and enthusiastic salesmen or woman is usually worth a lot to the company they work for because such energetic and positive people can easily sink their hooks into the emotions of their clients and have them follow them down an emotional rabbit-hole that leads them far from the realms of logic where they may easily lose a sale.

Watch out for this kind of approach. Someone coming across as enthusiastic and passionate about what they are speaking about may have that and nothing else. Keep such people focused on the facts and you could find yourself taking the dominant position in these kinds of discussions.

Charm

Charm, much like passion, is a common attribute a lot of the best salespeople in the game learn to master and weaponize. People are more likely to trust people they feel they get along with than they will someone they could not picture themselves enjoying an unrelated social interaction with.

This is one of the oldest tricks in the book as it makes you feel it is permissible to let down your guard and trust the individual in front of you. You do so at your own peril.

The Secret Techniques of the Best Leaders

Lead with the end in mind

The best leaders always have an agenda that they are trying to accomplish and that often determined their personal leadership style. They use their goals to determine what it will take to get them to where they want to go and how to keep people following them in that direction.

Since people are drawn to people who seem to have a clear vision of the path ahead, making your vision clear in necessary increments makes people more likely to follow them. Most people feel blind and lost, so the last person they want to follow is someone who is in the dark with them.

Use this knowledge to get others to fall for the allure of your seductive vision and they will follow you to the ends of the earth. Learning to see through the visions of charismatic leaders and asking how their vision helps you is a great way to make sure you never fall for the same spell yourself.

Selective generosity

Great leaders often know how to motivate their followers by creating a healthy sense of competition among those who work under them. One of the best strategies for accomplishing this is using selective generosity. Leaders who know how to complement and reward very carefully often have people feverishly toiling to earn the same spot in the sun.

It is best advised to do this sparsely and almost at random. Never show generosity too easily or the struggle to get it loses its value and you may find people not working with the same level of intensity you may require. Be too predictable about who, when or to whom you show generosity may make some feel isolated or that they may never be on the receiving end of this. To get the most out of this tactic, it is wise to ensure that people believe your gifts are plentiful and can reach the farthest ends of your domain and you will find yourself motivating even the grunts and scrubs who will probably never even get to see you.

Communication and honesty

Honesty is a good quality for any leader to have, but the best leaders understand that perception is everything so they remain selective with the information they share to everyone: friends, enemies or followers. It does not much matter who, but an air of complete honesty can be a great cover concealing your strengths and/or weaknesses.

It is good to remember that there is power in knowing when to appear vulnerable and when to appear strong, but it is always good for those who follow you to think you are always honest with them.

This can be achieved by picking moments where people feel like they can reach you and communicate with you if necessary, but you have to control this so it never works against or inconveniences you. Selectively opening your door to those you lead and knowing when to show weakness to them- but only when it can't be used against you- is a powerful tool in making people feel listened to and that they can trust you.

Motivate

Motivation and inspiration are the key qualities that can make or break a leader's run. While the dramatic, impassioned speech is what most people think of when they think of motivating people, it is a series of calculated actions that happen without people even realizing it.

Two great motivating factors are greed and fear. Yes, it is good to be loved where possible, but if being loved is impossible then you can always appeal to these two darker sides of people's personas.

Greed is simple enough. You want to make sure that you make every decision made feel like it benefits every party involved and then people will motivate themselves to chase the benefits they believe will come from following you.

Fear is a tightrope act to follow, but it works hand-in-hand with a sense of dependence. If you take time to make sure people you lead know that they need you and why, then the fear of being left alone in the wilderness to defend themselves will terrify them into action.

Boldness and confidence

One quality that often makes a lot of people feel they can trust in someone as a leader is seeing them succeed at taking risks. People often get put into a leadership position purely because they were seen going where no one has gone and lived to tell the tale. You can often see this in a lot of politicians especially. They can often make themselves seem like the shiny beacons guiding the country into and a brave new age of conquest or change.

This can be applied in everyday life. If you want people to follow you like so many often do, even when they are duped into voting for a bad presidential candidate, then you should be bold and confident in whatever actions you take and people will be drawn to your courage. They will want to be like you and stick around you in the hopes that they will absorb some of your boldness and ability to get what you want.

Reputation is everything

Perception is everything in the game of manipulation and persuasion. You never want to be seen in a light that makes you seem like anything other than what you want people to believe you are. Too many leaders lose their power just because they did not keep their hands clean and got caught in a scandal.

If you plan on leading, then always make sure that whatever unsavory actions you need to take are never taken in view of the public where your public perception can be tarnished and your reign ruined. Everything from your actions to your clothes must be a message to those around you, an illusion that tells whatever story you want to be told about you.

If you must do something that might put your reputation at risk, then it is best to make sure to give the public something else to look at while you do what you need to do and be swift enough to be finished by the time the distraction has lost its hold of their attention.

Delegation

The best leaders always know how much work they do not need to do themselves. It does not matter if they can do something better. Wasting time trying to do everything will eventually take away from the goals they strive towards. Delegation saves a lot of time and also has a slightly more sinister potential use. One can always use delegation as a means of getting credit for work they did not do.

Taking all the credit will obviously have negative consequences in the future as more and more people get tired of having credit for their work stolen from them. Taking all the credit is short-sighted. Instead, a good leader shares credit in everything they delegate to those among them.

Taking a little credit for everyone's work saves your time while boosting your worth in the eyes of others.

Discipline

Discipline is a two-edged blade. Great leaders often come across as being the most driven and disciplined people in the company, whether that is true or not. It often serves as a great inspiration to others to keep working hard as well. The other side of that comes when it is time to discipline others.

This can be a great way to keep people in line. Disciplining others should at times be a spectacle that might make others second guess their own ill-gotten intentions.

This is best used when enemies are crushed

completely and their punishment is meted out at by a leader who is justified for being hard on those who work against them or do not work to their required standard.

This is a double-edged sword in the sense that it relies on everyone knowing the standard set ahead of time and seeing it be met by the leader. Coldly crushing those who would not meet this standard is a good way to ensure that people fear the very idea of falling out of your good graces.

See adversity as an opportunity

One of the best ways leaders keep themselves and those around them motivated is by making sure they view setbacks as opportunities in disguise. There is nothing that boosts morale than a leader that seems to see the silver lining in every setback and communicates it well.

The very best of leaders never let their follower see them sweat unless it is a calculated move that serves a purpose. They take on the appearance of a solutions-based mindset and surround themselves with people who see things in a similar way.

Ideas are as contagious as any disease. Make the idea of you being unperturbed by stormy seas and those loyal to you will bravely follow you wherever you choose to lead them. Even if it has to be faked, never let those around you see you stressed or pressured under adversity and you will win their admiration and loyalty.

The Secret Techniques of the Best Public Speakers

Prepare to make it seem effortless

The last thing you ever see good public speakers doing is trying to be good. They speak as if they are not bothered by where they are or who they are speaking to. It seems completely natural. This is how they win even the toughest of crowds over.

What the audience seldom sees is the hours checking the venue and equipment to make sure nothing plays against them or malfunctions on the day; the hours of rehearsing the speech and gestures so it all seems random and spontaneous on stage; the affirmations and other relaxation and motivation exercises.

They only see the finished product and that truth on the stage is the only one that matters to them; they never see behind the illusion.

Making mistakes

Most of the time you find that few to none of the people in the audience ever really know what the speech is supposed to sound like, so there's no point in worrying about making the odd mistake. Great speakers know these two things: 1) the audience is on your side; 2) the mistakes you make on stage are almost never as big, noticeable or memorable as you imagine they'll be.

This is great for helping with nerves, making sure that you don't dwell on the mistakes when you make them, and keep moving forward. Move on as you would in everyday conversation and the audience will soon forget about whatever mistakes you made.

Think about talking, not making a speech

Once great speakers are done with their preparation, they no longer feel the need to actively think about making a good speech. They know that muscle memory will soon kick in and things will come naturally as if they were on autopilot.

A part of this happens in the preparation phases but is vital to remember before hitting the stage as well. The best speakers often make it seem as if their speech is part of an ordinary conversation. The most impressive elements of the speech happen in the preparation/practice phases of the speech. What happens on stage is simply the by-product of this, so there's usually nothing to worry about at this point.

Personalize the message

Some of the best and most captivating speeches are often the ones that tie in with a personal story or two. People love stories and nothing better communicates why the content of your speech is important than a story about why it's important to you.

Stories are often easier to remember than facts, so punctuating a fact-dense speech with enjoyable stories regarding or including those facts will not only make them more memorable but will also add a level of sincerity to the speech that most people just can't fake. Don't be afraid to add a touch of authenticity to your stories by lacing them with a personal story here and there.

Start with the end in mind

Few things are more annoying than speeches that seem to take forever to get to the point. Top public speakers know that by the time they get to the point, the audience will be lost to them. Regaining the audience's attention once it's gone is very tricky to do and often not worth the risk, irrespective of how good the point of the speech actually was.

It is far better to start with the point and then build the speech around it. Regardless of the topic of your speech, you want to make sure never to risk the point of it being lost to the audience at any point.

Leave them wanting more

There is absolutely nothing wrong with wanting to leave everything on the stage and leaving the audience in awe of you. Unfortunately, this is not a concert you're headlining. If you watch your favorite public speakers closely enough, you will notice that they often leave the speech at a place that feels like a good logical conclusion without having people ever feel like they were getting tired of listening to them speaking.

The best way to never have the audience tire of listening to a speech is to ensure that the same things are repeated in different ways as often as possible. Becoming too repetitive, though necessary, becomes boring and tiring once the pattern of repetitiveness is predictable and/or uninteresting.

Engage the audience

The best speakers on the planet tend to make a talk feel more like a fun conversation than a full-on presentation of ideas. They do this by engaging the audience using things like eye-contact and, sometimes, audience participation.

Looking down at one's notes can be tempting to avoid facing the audience and seeing something that might make you feel self-conscious. Avoid this at all cost. Instead, go around the venue, with your eyes, talking to people individually for a few seconds. This will make them feel they need to give their utmost attention.

Asking the audience questions where possible (it doesn't matter if they're rhetorical at times) can make the audience feel like they are a vital part of the speech and so need to keep listening close in case they have to answer questions as individuals or a group.

Watch body language

Make it a point to watch some of the speeches of your favorite speakers with the volume all the way down someday. You will probably notice that you can still feel the emotions the speakers are trying to convey without you hearing the words. This is because the best public speakers are very aware of the power of their bodies to sub-communicate their message so they use it to their fullest.

They know they run the risk of giving away some of their private thoughts through their body language so they actively seek to control it instead. This not only enhances their talk but also aids whatever illusion they are trying to keep going while on stage.

Confidence

You probably hear this all the time, but one can never state enough how vital it is to do things with as much confidence as humanly possible. Confidence is not a natural trait for a lot of people, but there are some ways to overcome that.

The majority of one's confidence will often come from having security in their preparation. Knowing that you did everything you logically could to prevent things from going wrong will give a boost to even the most neurotic of people. There are still some other methods to consider if this is not enough though.

Making use of things like hypnosis, meditation, legal drugs, affirmations etc. can be your best friend if you struggle with nerves more than most people.

Simplify the message

If you were invited to give a speech somewhere then there is a good chance that people already respect your authority on that subject. This means that there is no need to go writing a speech that is filled with jargon or other difficult language to understand.

Truly great public speakers will do their best to mold their speeches to the audiences so that no one is lost. It is more important to be understood than it is to impress. This is common knowledge among the best public speakers. They are not afraid to let the content they are presenting to the impressing while they focus on making sure their talk is engaging and understood.

Congruency

Giving a speech is every as much a viewing experience as it is a listening one. As such, it is important that an orator make it a point that their bodies and voice match every part of their speech.

They look and sound excited when they say something they consider exciting. They sound bored when they say something they consider boring. They will even laugh when saying something they consider funny.

This is congruence, letting the effects of one's words show in the face, body and voice. A lack of congruency can add an element of detachment that might give the impression that there isn't any need to pay attention to your words, ruining what could have been a great speech.

Be passionate

This is probably another point that is stated too often, but that does not make it any less true. Having a passion for the subject at hand pouring out of a speaker can have an almost hypnotic effect. The only thing that might match this kind of intensity is the energy that comes from a person giving a speech visibly fighting going off the rails because the topic they're speaking about them fills them with that much emotion and energy. This alone can make a speech so engrossing that forgetting it is no longer an option.

If you ever find yourself in a position where you have to make a speech, make sure it is about something you feel very strongly about or at least approach it in such a way that you end up feeling so strongly about it and your audience will reward you for it.

Chapter 2: Dark Psychology 101 - The Principles of Dark Psychology:

Dark psychology has many different aspects and elements that encompass it. While it is true that we all have these elements within us to some degree, we are not all prone to using them all the time. Most of us will use them when we feel there is no other course for us to take, so we get manipulative.

Ordinary people prefer not to deceive or manipulate. They will usually lean towards doing things in a more honest way and try their best not to hurt those around them. They will eventually go dark if they feel they were pushed into using these techniques. However, not everyone operates like this.

There are people who, for various reasons that aren't always obvious, will dive straight into these tactics as their go-to. They can be for our own good at times, but they often aren't. They will use these tricks on unsuspecting people regardless of the effects they might have on them.

You will often find, as it will be discussed in later chapters, that the kinds of people who actively use the techniques of dark psychology will usually have morals that don't match those most people might follow. These are usually people who are damaged and live their lives expressing their inner demons in toxic ways. However, there are those who will use dark psychology because they are what can be considered cold-hearted or even evil. They usually have no regard for the wellbeing of other people whatsoever.

This chapter will give you some insight into how these people may behave. While explanations of what may drive them will come later, chapter 2 will give you some insight into how they go about their business. What are some of the most common tactics you will find people using on you in contexts that may have nothing to do with your work? Some of them might be used on you in your social life.

The hope is that deeper insight into these tools that have probably been used against most people, will allow them to know what to look out for and perhaps react accordingly. The other hope is that it may help people use them to change their lives for the better in various aspects of their lives be it in their careers, their education, their social lives, or even their love lives.

Benign/Covert

Reverse psychology

This is perhaps one of the most well-known and possibly clichéd forms of dark psychology. The main reason it can be considered benign, or non-threatening is that so many people know this method that it is really not that difficult to spot.

However, it can be a powerful tool when used right. It is most likely to work against very stubborn people who are always likely to do the exact opposite of what they are told. With this in mind, one begins to understand why telling them to do the opposite of what you desire them to do will most likely move in the direction you actually want them to.

This method is also a great way to disguise your intentions and make it seem as if the target acted of their own free will.

Love flooding

This insidious method is one of the most difficult methods to detect, especially when used subtly enough and in conjunction with reinforcement and withdrawal/denial.

Love flooding (sometimes known as love bombing) is when a predator suddenly showers a potential victim with gifts, praise and positivity. Love flooding can be dangerous because it can be used to disguise sadistic motivations behind positive actions sustained for a calculated amount of time.

How it works is that one would use this technique to have their intended victim subconsciously associate them with positive feelings. Once a dependency has been established and the wanted rapport is created, it becomes a lot easier to get the target to do as the persuader wants them to.

This method works best at the beginning of the relationship when trust is still in the process of being built.

Reinforcement

Used correctly (usually as a follow up from love flooding/bombing) this very covert tool can be used to create an almost Pavlovian behavior in a target.

It is easy to think that the work ends when the love flooding has done its job. However there needs to be another rung on the ladder that leads to getting what one wants or interest may wane before the original desire of the persuader is met.

By restricting one's affection, attention and praise for when someone does as the manipulator pleases, it creates a deep desire in the victim to do whatever it is that will make them feel good again. The target will soon behave in the required manner in order to get the positive reinforcement they believe they can get only from you.

Love withdrawal/denial

This step may seem a little counter-intuitive, but there is a lot of good reasoning behind using a tactic like this. It is a great follow up after love flooding/bombing and then reinforcement.

Once a person, say a potential love interest, for example, has already started associating the persuader with feelings of positivity and little reward has to be given to elicit that response, then occasionally withdrawing or denying love can be a powerful closer.

It simply creates an air of unpredictability around the manipulator while giving them complete control of the mind and emotions of their victim.

This is achieved by 'randomly' giving rewards for required behavior where the reward was given every time the desired behavior was shown. It keeps the victim guessing about the state of mind of the manipulator while increasingly making them crave the old attention they came to expect from them.

Passive aggressiveness:

Guilt tripping: it is a very common way for people trying to avoid a direct confrontation to get what they want without risking an undesirable outcome.

It heavily relies on making a person feel bad by bringing up something they did, said, or even implied. It doesn't even matter if it actually happened. What's important is that they feel swayed by their guilt to lowering their guard enough to be nudged in the right direction.

Sarcasm: this is another tactic for getting the desired response without risking a direct confrontation because sarcasm is often used in a humorous way.

Sarcasm can be used to deliver biting words in a funny way without giving the victim reasonable cause to flare up and get confrontational without looking like the ones in the wrong.

This works especially well in public areas where the one who seems to be in the wrong might call on the judgement and/or wrath of an on-looking crowd.

Bribery

This can take many forms and will not be as salacious as one would imagine if done right.

The trick to this is never being seen to be the one offering the bribe, but rather getting the other party to ask or even expect the bribe.

This works best if it started off as simply rewarding/reinforcing good behavior so that one is never suspected of bribing, but simply cashing in on the favor they have built up over time.

It can come in the form of small gifts, money, favors, etc. It doesn't matter. What does matter is that they align with the needs of the person who is to be bribed.

This can be tricky to accomplish in the heat of the moment if favor hasn't been garnered over time, but can slowly be built up to if one is patient, compliant, and is willing to ask questions that seem innocuous while actually looking for the weak spot where a need can be met.

Deception:

Lying: while most people are not as good as lying as they think they are, it is not uncommon for people we meet every day to try anyway, just to be given away by their body language, if one knows where to look.

Half-truths: while these are easier to pull off, they can be trickier to remember as they can weave a story that's too difficult to navigate under pressure.

Exaggeration: blowing the truth out of proportion to some degree can be a good way to get what you want or get out of trouble, but is difficult to get out of it if caught red-handed.

Diminishing: downplaying the truth can be just as difficult as exaggerating, but can be a good way to delay trouble while looking for an escape route.

Omission: leaving out facts in a story is easily a favorite of many persuaders as the blame can be placed on the victim if anything goes wrong.

Fraud: this is the drawn up act of creating an elaborate scheme to get one's way, but the consequences of it can far outweigh the good, in most cases.

Implication: this entails using certain words just to claim one may have a different understanding of those words if questioned later. It offers plausible deniability.

Yes-stacking

'Yes-stacking' is simply asking someone a series of questions they are most likely to answer yes to. Once they have done this more than three times in a row, it becomes easier to ask them for what you really want as most humans feel a strong need to seem congruent with themselves. So if someone suddenly answers 'no' after having answered in the affirmative so many times they can end up answering yes just to avoid the discomfort of feeling, or even seeming incongruent with themselves.

Slightly harder cases can often be leaned on with a bit of guilt by reminding them of their own words and this will further trigger their innate need to seem congruent to themselves and others. Yes-stacking is often used by a lot of people in the sales industry to 'close' the sale with a customer.

Subliminal influence:

Visual: this is the method of using images, often in subtle ways, to get certain ideas into someone's mind without them suspecting that they are being manipulated.

Carefully placing an object, color, or image that triggers certain feelings where they'll be visible without being obvious will ingrain those feelings in a deeply subconscious way. This can be seen anywhere from presidents (and presidential candidates) wearing specifically colored neckties, to an everyday person placing an object with a certain picture in the background of a video chat because one knows that it will subconsciously bring those feelings to the surface.

Audio: using this can be trickier to use on an individual, but can be very powerful to get them to do what one wants without their knowledge. Examples of this can be in Hollywood horror movies where the sound is used to set up something called a 'jump-scare'. The sounds themselves can create such an intense atmosphere that nothing scary actually has to happen on the screen for people to jump out of their seats. Marketers with memorable jingles in their adverts can use this to get people to think about their products long after the ad is over.

Dark persuasion

Unearthing need

Picking one's targets wisely will come up a lot in this book, but that is because the importance of it can never be stressed enough. One should never go for a bad target unless it the only target open for maneuver. Even then, it can be considered ill-advised and should be approached with extreme caution.

The best targets to go for are often ones who seem to have some kind of need that is within your power to meet. This need could be encouragement, companionship, intellectual stimulation, and the list goes on.

First identifying the needs of the target is wise because it tells the persuader a lot about what strategy to execute and perhaps even help fill in some of the details pertaining to how the said strategy may be approached.

The long game

Not to be confused with dark escalations, this technique can be used to erode someone's defenses over time and eventually see the manipulator getting their way.

It usually starts with identifying some need a target has and then using that as an entry point for infiltration and slowly building a strong bond with the potential victim.

It will then be built upon by earning the trust of the target. This is best achieved by getting them to trust your intentions and advice. A good way of doing this is occasionally getting them to do things that will benefit them without you getting anything in return. They will soon trust you implicitly.

At this point, it simply becomes about waiting for the right moment to get what it was you originally wanted from them (best approached with still hidden intentions). For example, asking them for some money you will surely pay back, or even invest for them.

Dark escalation

This can seem very similar to the long game. However, it differs in the fact that it often ends with a terrible ask at the end and the road to getting there can be somewhat different.

One usually seeks someone going through a difficult time and maybe in desperate need somehow. People like this are usually the easiest to get to fall for this tactic; think of the German people being roped into following Hitler into the extermination of the Jews and then World War II.

It starts with convincing someone, or a group of people, to trust the manipulator. Once they do, they ask them to go against their morals in the slightest of ways. Once they do and notice that there were no negative consequences, they will be more inclined to do something a little worse the next time.

With time, they will willingly commit almost any atrocity.

Disguising intentions

This may sound simple and obvious, but one would be surprised by how easy it is to get this wrong. The concept itself is more complex than most realize and involves a series of actions and a level of consistency that only the most accomplished manipulators ever pull off.

One of the things that are needed to get this right is approaching situations indirectly. Imagine a persuader approaching a potential love interest at a bar. Walking up to them may seem a bit intimidating or desperate. Approaching them from behind seems creepy since the target might feel like they were snuck up on and that may trigger some paranoia. The skilled manipulator will instead approach from an angle that is within eyesight without being too head on.

This example can be used when considering any situation where one might try to get someone to do something they normally would not.

Fatigue Inducement

Although this strategy can be pretty easy to see when known about, there are some contexts where it can be hidden enough to disguise its intention.

Most people might be familiar with law enforcement officers or even lawyers using it to wear down the mental faculties of someone they want to interrogate. They might keep them awake for long periods of time until they feel frustrated enough to answer any and all questions in the desired fashion.

Another example of this that is easily missed is when salespeople use it on customers by pretending to go around asking questions to the relevant parties while they keep you waiting as you slowly become more frustrated and just want to get out of there.

Leading questions

This technique distracts the target from all the choices they have by framing questions in a specific way. For example, rather than asking someone if they want to eat at home or not, they are asked where they would love to go out for food instead.

The person being persuaded often doesn't realize that they are being distracted from thinking too much about the choice of eating at home and instead are being drawn to thinking about where to eat out.

This does not give them a yes or no answer, nor does it present them all the options they actually have before them. They are instead made to answer an open-ended question that aligns their answer with that of the persuader, if done right. You will often see attorneys using this kind of method when questioning a witness.

Choice restriction

This technique may be very similar to using leading questions, but the subtle differences make it a formidable tool that can stand on its own. Choice restriction, much like leading questions, is used to keep the target from taking too much time considering all the options at their feet. However, it differs in giving the target a set of closed options that they favor the persuader.

A good example of this would be someone asking a person they are trying to ask out on a date if they should meet up for drinks or a meal, rather than flat out asking if they would like to go out on a date with them.

In this example, one sees how the target is given a false sense of agency when they are really being put between a rock and a hard place.

Emotional transference

Emotional transference is a tool that is as versatile as it is effective. Manipulation is often about using emotions to overcome someone's logic. This technique is the embodiment of that idea.

It is best done using voice and body language to get someone onto your plane of thought without ever realizing it.

Manipulators may start by assessing the current tone and body language of their victim and mimic them to falsely match their state of mind. Once this is done, the victim is then tested to see if they will unconsciously mimic the actions and/or tone mood of the manipulator.

The tests can be as subtle as folding one's arms to see if the target will adopt this position or stay in their own.

Mimicry will tell the persuader of the target's willingness to comply.

Gas-lighting

This is possibly one of the most insidious tactics that will be covered in this chapter. It involves slowly chipping away at someone's very sanity. It's simple to understand, but difficult to carry out and can have devastating effects on the victim it is being practiced on.

It involves denying simple realities that the victim is sure of. It's best to do this with subtle things that the victim might be a little fuzzy on.

Once this has been done a few times, the victim comes to accept that their manipulator simply has a better memory than they do. Unfortunately, things don't stop there.

The number and gravity of the 'forgotten' or 'confused' incidents begins to gradually increase until the victim begins to doubt their very sanity.

With time, the victim comes to trust the mental fortitude of their manipulator more than their own and become completely dependent on them.

Mind games

Playing hard to get

Playing hard to get is closely related to love denial, but is not exactly the same thing. The biggest difference to take note of is that playing hard to get can happen at the beginning phase of a healthy relationship, romantic or not. The dark version of playing hard to get on the other hand involves doing so while the relationship is already in progress.

This dark tactic also differs from love withdrawal in the way it uses withdrawal. Love withdrawal/denial often uses specific behaviors to withdraw from the target. Playing hard to get, on the other hand, can go as far as removing one's entire presence from the victim to create a sense of anxiety in them, making them desperate to get back the person they sense is pulling away from them.

Finger pointing

This is a method that is most likely to be used by children and people with certain borderline personality disorders. You will often find that they are likely to try to point fingers to make it seem like they are not at fault for something even if they are caught red-handed. They will try their hardest to make it seem that someone or something else is at fault for their misdeeds, even the person blaming them.

One of the most common ways they do this is by pointing out that someone else is worse than them or blame it on human nature. They will do anything to get out of trouble Scott-free. Learning to spot the application of this can be more useful than learning to use it to get out of trouble.

Playing the victim

This is very similar to finger pointing except that it uses guilt as the means to escape. While a degree of finger pointing is used to avoid receiving blame, the real purpose of this technique is to use guilt to paint the persuader as the victim of something they themselves were unable to control.

Doing this can be as easy as pointing out that one was merely the agent of some variable or factor that they could not control. This can imply that one was deceived, misled or confused by some force they could not control.

Doing this can be handy in a pinch, but it is best used as a way of buying time rather than a fix-all strategy for getting out of some trouble. Relying on this alone leaves one exposed to being caught if a simple interrogation of the facts takes place.

Ultimatums

It is important to realize that ultimatums can be broken up into light and dark ones. The distinction is small but crucial. This will determine whether it is successfully used by you or on you.

Light ultimatums will often benefit both parties or just the person it is being offered to. An example of this is when someone is asked to stop a bad habit or pick up a good one for their own sake or the sake of the relationship(s) in their lives regardless of whether they are romantic or not.

Dark ultimatums, however, do not take into account the wellbeing of the person they are being offered to. They will usually ask someone to violate their own conscience for some reason. It can take the form of trying to pressure someone to do something that may harm them on some level or risk being mocked, shunned, ostracized, etc.

The eternal breakup

Implied breakup: making use of crafty language to make someone think a breakup in a relationship has happened, just to turn around and act like nothing is wrong. This crafty tool is hard to deal with because it offers such a high degree of plausible deniability.

Promised breakup: the promised break up will hang the idea of an impending break up in order to get someone to behave a certain way. By making them unsure of the longevity of the relationship, they will be filled with anxiety and become much easier to control.

Fake breakup: this is a somewhat extreme method to prove a point or get a reaction. It involves literally breaking up with someone without the intention of actually ending the relationship. So one might choose to start a fight and then pack their bags and say they're leaving, just to end up staying.

Status games

Status games can come in many forms and use a lot of techniques to make someone believe that a manipulator is of a higher social status than a certain person or group of people. This can involve using big words or numbers and statistics to make themselves seem more intelligent than they really are. Even the simple use of body language can be part of these status games.

It all relies on subtlety and making sure that one never overplays their hand. It can be easy to catch out someone who uses this method by asking them to define these large words they like using or asking them to state their source regarding some of the facts and statistics they like quoting so much. This tactic should be used sparingly and with great caution.

Seek insecurities

Now, this is a skill many manipulators will use to better understand how to maneuver someone in the direction that they want without being too obvious about it.

They can pay very close attention and make sure to get as much information as possible out of a person while giving as little as they can about themselves. Just remember that this is not about boosting one's ego. It is simply gaining sensitive information on someone so they will be easier to handle.

Take care not to feel too superior after receiving this information or your body language may give you away. It takes something as small as a tiny grin or a glint of joy in one's eye to give away the whole game, so school your emotions and control your expressions to help conceal your real game.

Slander

Expert users of the techniques of dark psychology can use slander like a well-crafted tool to gain control of some unsuspecting person. They never do it purely for emotional reasons. Rather it is employed as a necessary means to gain and/or maintain control.

Slander can be used to eat away at the reputation and/or credibility of a certain target for various reasons. If used subtly enough, it can be used to make someone run to the manipulator for comfort or council even though they may have been the ones to have started the rumor. It can also be useful for getting troublesome parties out of the way or at least slow them down enough for the manipulator to gain the upper hand over them.

People often get caught trying to use this to boost their own self-image by destroying the perception of others, but that is a slippery slope that can easily backfire since the slander seem like its own end.

Manipulating negativity

Since most people often shy away from conflict, it can be very useful to regain control of tricky situations by controlling the negativity. Dark persuaders will do this by putting someone on the back foot by making a simple interaction tense by taking on a negative body language, tone of voice, etc.

A simple conversation can turn into a screaming match just so that the manipulator does not have to account for their actions. They can act depressed or shattered by something that happened, even if it is not real, just to avoid a serious conversation about the real issue at hand or at least try to control the outcome of the one they are having.

Flooding negative emotions can often work to offset someone who is justifiably upset by becoming just as upset or worse and making them believe someone else (or they themselves) are actually in the wrong.

Brainwashing

Isolation

This is usually the first step in the process of any brainwashing. Taking a victim away from anything familiar to them leaves them more vulnerable to having their identities dissolved and replaced with new ones.

Whether it is in a cult, war camp, or an abusive relationship, isolation will be the first part as it becomes a lot more difficult to make decisions based on a victim's old self when they are far away from anything or anyone that may give them the strength to stand up for themselves or question anything that is presented to them.

While some of these steps will not always happen in the exact same sequence, this is one that is usually done first before any of the real brainwashing can begin.

Mental abuse

The subject is often forced to do or say embarrassing things in order to wear down their self-esteem and make them more malleable.

The mental abuse is one of many tactics that are designed to bring the victim to their knees and eventually have a mental breakdown once their old identity feels completely shattered. After they have had a mental breakdown, their minds are for the taking.

Mental abuse can come in a lot of different forms that may be verbal or non-verbal. It can involve anything from making the victim believe everything they do is wrong to constantly humiliating them in private and/or public.

Physical abuse

Depending on the scenario, physical abuse can be a powerful tool for breaking down the mental state of a victim of brainwashing and cults. While it is not a necessary element in a one-on-one situation, it can often be seen being used in cults or war prisons.

The abuse can be anything from sexual assault to physical torture or even beatings. What matters above all else is that the victim is subjected to constant physical and psychological pain if they are to be properly broken down and expected to make extreme changes in their ideological beliefs and way of life. After enough of this, the victim will be willing to do almost anything to experience relief.

Scare tactics

There are few tools that can lead to the mental breakdown of a victim than constant uncertainty that something bad may happen to them at any time. The constant anxiety creates an existential despair that can cause some serious psychological and physical symptoms to manifest.

Weeks or months of this treatment can lead to panic attacks, depression, heart palpitations, reduced health and vitality, etc.

Fatigue and malnourishment

This is a common first step one will notice happens in a lot of cults, prisons of war or sometimes even functions related to large corporations trying to get people to spend more money than they intended or just take worse deals than they normally would have. This usually happens at the beginning of the brain-washing, but can be used again in later stages. Cults will often make their members go on fasts just to reinforce the indoctrination.

This can happen in multiple ways from sleep deprivation to limiting meals or even making victims eat meals that are low in the necessary nutrients to keep them energetic and aware, making them less suggestible than a manipulator might desire.

Guilt

Guilt is a powerful tool that is used in multiple ways during the brainwashing of a victim. It uses a multitude of weapons against the victim such as: self-criticism and finger pointing; getting the victim to do or say things that fill them with guilt, like renouncing their friends and family; constantly yelling at or beating the victim so they feel that anything they say, think or do is just wrong; accusing them of wrong or past sins from the life they had before being found by the manipulator. The list goes on.

After feeling enough guilt for long enough, a victim's mind will slowly deteriorate and have them agonizing for some form of escape from their own minds.

Self-betrayal

Getting a victim to betray themselves is difficult and takes time, but is an essential part of brain-washing. This will not happen in the initial phases of the brainwashing, but later when the victim is broken (or close to it) and is desperate for some form of relief.

Asking the victim to betray themselves in some small way gives the victim a little hope that the torture will eventually stop while bringing them ever closer to the edge of their sanity. It needs to happen in increments though, like asking them to confess to past sins and eventually building up to having them denounce their old life and identity.

Leniency

This is an essential part of any brain-washing regardless of the context. Whether it happens in an abusive relationship or in a cult, it is important that the victim eventually get the occasional reprieve. This can happen in the form of asking them what they miss most about their old life; showing them some small gesture of affection or kindness; giving them a short break where they are treated somewhat humanely, etc.

The odd showing of leniency (weeks or months into the brain-washing) will make the victim, whose thoughts are being wired, feel the urge to return the favor somehow. It will help ingrain the sense of indebtedness to the manipulators even though they are directly responsible for their current suffering.

Non-consensual hypnosis

Repetitive music: this is a crafty trick because if the beat is at a speed close enough to that of the human heart then it can slowly put the victim into an almost trancelike state that makes them far more suggestible.

With time, the music will change the victim's brain waves so they are easier to persuade.

Chanting and singing: the use of constant chanting or singing (which usually takes place once the victim has been allowed to meet the other members of a group.

The constant singing and chanting with the group creates a sense of oneness with the group while further ingraining the doctrines of the manipulator.

Identity assassination

This is when the manipulators will tear down everything the victim used to believe to be true from them. Their old life is made to seem wrong and immoral. It is indicated as being the source of all of the victim's current suffering. Everything related to that character is slowly taken from the victim so that they may be 'cleansed' and given an opportunity to end their suffering, by denouncing their old life and everyone from it.

In some case, as with certain cults and even terrorist organizations, the victim is being prepared to be 'reborn' where they are even given a new name to match their new identity.

Love bombing

This is similar to love flooding, except it is usually reserved for the end of the process and used to help the victim feel they are part of the fold and entering a blissful new life. This often happens in the form of ceremony but is not always necessary.

The victim is given lots of attention and affection so that they may feel welcome to the group and part of something good. This will so greatly contrast the pain and suffering they previously endured that it will further ingrain the feeling of dependency on the people who brainwashed them. Their natural desire to be accepted will override logic and make them not even want to consider leaving.

Chapter 3: The Dark Triad

What is the dark triad?

The dark triad may sound like something out of a Hollywood movie, but it is actually the cornerstone of dark psychology and, by extension, this book. The dark triad refers to the three personality types that inspired the inception of dark psychology. In fact, these three personality types are where the techniques found in dark psychology stems from. What are these big three that are the basis for a field of study that may seem so bizarre then?

The three personality types that make up the dark triad, while seemingly self-explanatory, can be difficult to spot because of some unfortunate misunderstandings about their nature and origin. The dark triad consists of: Machiavellianism, Narcissism and Psychopathy. While these may seem to paint pictures that give them away off the bat, it is often not quite that simple.

People associate Machiavellianism with a political type who took 'The Prince' a little too seriously; Narcissism as someone who is enamored with their own image; and a Psychopath as someone straight out of a slasher film. The real-life examples of these traits are more sinister than that as they can easily slip under the radar and operate under the veil of the general public's ignorance.

The dark triad is associated with personality traits that show a strong link to Borderline Personality Disorder (BPD). Most people may find that they manifest at least some of the qualities represented on the dark triad, but people who have very high concentrations of one part of the triad or even some combination of the three can be terribly destructive forces in any given aspect of everyday life.

The purpose of this chapter is to help build an understanding of the dark triad so that one may be better able to spot them and avoid being sucked into their games of deception and betrayal. Though they are not always so easy to spot, there are some ways to identify what makes these people who they are, even without the battery of psychological tests necessary to spot them definitively.

Machiavellianism

What is Machiavellianism?

This specific character trait interests most people because it has its roots, at least in part, in a work of political philosophy written by the diplomat and political philosopher, Niccolo Machiavelli, in the Renaissance era. While imprisoned, he wrote a book detailing all the principles he deemed necessary for rulers and would be rulers to acquire and retain power. This was sent to the ruler at the time in the hopes that it would buy him some favor in the eyes of price Di Medici.

This book became the blueprint used by politicians and those who might rule over people in a broad and impactful fashion. While most people have some of these Machiavellian traits, they will seldom act on them too often. The true Machiavellian does not care about moderating these behaviors. They will, in fact, live by them as if by some philosophical code for their lives.

It is interesting to note that this is one of the easiest traits for most people to adopt and benefit from, despite being a symptom of mental illness. People can be born with this trait though, but the evidence that supports this is rare. More often than not, people high in Machiavellianism (high Machs) are more likely to have been made this way by having been subjected to a childhood that involved a cold style of parenting and everything seemed conditional at best.

High Machs, are master manipulators capable of ruining the lives of many while having the potential to teach many about those who play games of power and how to handle yourself around them. It does not matter whether one intends to learn about them out of curiosity; to deal with them in some sphere of life; or adopt some of their habits as their own to get what they want from life. These people offer a lot of wisdom to offer anyone willing to learn.

How does the High Mach operate?

Like all three of the personality types on the dark triad, the Machiavellian is often insanely charming. They know how to charm their way into or around any social situation to get what they want. All that matters to them is usually that they get what they want by any means necessary. They can be terribly selfish people with very little or no sense of morality or remorse.

One of the easiest example to conjure up of this person is the character, Iago, from Shakespeare's "Othello". High Machs, like Iago, are cunning and very manipulative, using anyone or anything to help them get the advantages they want and feel they deserve. They will cunningly operate from the shadows and show surprising amounts of patience because the end result matters more than anything else to them. The only thing that might matter as much as the end result to a High Mach, is their reputation.

Reputation to someone high in Machiavellianism, is king. There is no better way of not getting caught out as a deceiving manipulator than having a pristine reputation. Think of politicians and/or businessmen who get found out for having been involved in some scandalous affair or dodgy dealing long after they were dead or retired. These are the kinds of people who hid their sordid personas behind the impeccable reputation. Machiavellians tend to be drawn to the long game because they often consider their goals to be more important than human relationships, so they have few to no real personal attachments to hold them back.

High Machs are often so dedicated to their own interests that people around them only exist on two sides of the same coin: those who benefit me and those who do not. People are just a tool for them to use and manipulate to their own end. Get in their way though and they will deal with you ruthlessly as they have little to no remorse and are cynical by nature, not believing in any inherent goodness in people.

What can be taken away from the Machiavellian?

While most people might not be high in trait Machiavellianism, there is a lot we can learn from this leg of the dark triad. It has some elements to it that ordinary people can learn from in order to get what they want or at least live more peaceful lives where they are not constantly being taken advantage of. That last part speaks more to people who are very low on the Machiavellian scale and tend to be too 'nice' or agreeable.

The potential to build a better life in many respects is found in this part of the dark triad if one knows what to look out for and use wisely. There are many bad aspects to being a high Mach, but there are some great advantages to being willing to learn from this type of person. At the very least, one should be able to know enough to identify if they are part of some elaborate game that they might be forced to pay for later on.

Patience and reputation are among the biggest things one can take away from the Machiavellian. Loathed to investing in short cuts, the Machiavellian teaches us that patience is key when climbing the ladder of power and success. They behave like predators, claws and teeth ever ready to strike in an instant, but patiently waiting for the right moment to pounce while concealing themselves as they wait.

People are also important, so learning how to pick and choose the right targets so that the rise to the top is made faster is crucial. It should be noted though that the best way to attain that trust is to make sure that one's reputation is kept spotless. If something underhanded must be done, then find someone to do it for you while you keep your nose clean. A good reputation will do a lot of your persuading for you.

Narcissism

What is Narcissism?

Narcissism is one of those traits that are easy to

miss since we are constantly surrounded by it. This is compounded by the fact that we live in a world that seems to reward narcissism even in its darkest form. This is not just a trait that makes people fall in love with taking pictures of themselves. That is the watered-down, diet version that has a low negative impact on most people. The darker type can lead to abuse, bullying, sabotage, and a whole host of consequences for the narcissist and anyone who might cross their path.

Although it can be classified as a mental disorder, or at least a part or symptom of one, it can be very difficult to spot, even for professionals. It can disguise itself in a number of ways and take many shapes and forms. These different types of narcissism will be broken down so that the reader may better filter out the everyday, run-of-the-mill narcissism from the potentially toxic and dark kind.

Grandiose narcissist- This type of narcissist is the classical image of what one may expect to see when thinking about this leg of the dark triad. This is someone who wears the finest clothes they possibly can, whether they can afford it or not; they have massive egos; they are entitled to the point where it borders on psychopathic; they are obsessed with how people see them, etc.

This kind of narcissist may seem like less of a danger because they are so easy to spot, but do not be fooled. These people tend to be very charming and charismatic. Their grandiose way of approaching things give them a false air of confidence that draws people to them. It also doesn't help much that they seem can be pretty generous when the mood takes them.

This is not to be taken lightly. These people are expert manipulators with an unbelievable lack of empathy, like everyone else in the dark triad. Moreover, they are far more insecure than they seem and will fly into a rage the second they feel they are being criticized. They will tear down your reputation or try to destroy you if they feel this will restore their fragile egos.

Malignant narcissist- These are the kind of narcissist you will most likely want to keep the closest eye on. They can have a streak that far exceeds all the other types of narcissists and can easily be mistaken for psychopaths. They will also have terribly grand ideas of themselves, like all narcissists, even if there is no evidence of said grandiosity.

These are the kind of narcissist who get so obsessed with the constant dreams of power and status all narcissists have that they will do whatever it takes to attain them. They are far more likely to cross moral boundaries to get what they want and expect everyone to see them as being justified in all they do because they are simply getting what is owed to them. They are the most likely to *expect* special treatment and favors from everyone.

When you combine these elements with the signature traits of having little to no empathy, plus their insane ambition mixed in with their skills of manipulation, and you have a walking powder keg just waiting to explode and ruin countless lives to achieve what they believe they deserve. People like this will do things most moral people with a conscious would not consider doing while in their right mind, so crossing their path must be done with extreme caution if it can't be avoided altogether.

Covert narcissist- the narcissist can be the trickiest of the lot to spot since they can often make people feel sorry for them in how they present their narcissism. While caring for people just as little as other narcissists, they are very good at making people see them as the victim of circumstances they could not control.

They will speak a lot about how smart, talented, or generally superior they are in some way. They will place the blame for their lack of success on politics, geography, or even being born at the wrong time. They will come across as someone who had everything going for them in a world that had something against them.

These types of people will often be misdiagnosed as being depressed and people will want to feel sorry for them. This would be a mistake as these kinds of people are prone to being insanely passive aggressive. However, being afraid of conflict is not their only reason for being this way. They consider themselves superior and enjoy playing games with the people in their lives. They can build themselves up by slowly breaking you down and bringing you into their world where they can feed off your negativity. Of course, the void they are trying to fill has no bottom, so people can get stuck trying to save these people until they have nothing more to give, just to be thrown away for someone who has something to give.

Communal narcissist- now communal narcissists are the kind of people who love to do good things. They will feed the homeless, take care of abandoned animals, shelter the needy, go for events that benefit others, etc. This doesn't sound too bad right? Think again. These are the kinds of people who will do a lot of good things, but absolutely have to be seen doing them or there simply isn't any point for them to be doing them.

They lack empathy just as much as the next narcissist, but they also need praise just as much as any other narcissist. This is why they do the altruistic things they do. They're in it for the ego boost that comes with the praise they receive for doing these things. Inwardly, they still have the same sense of superiority that comes with this character trait and it will often show without them knowing. They can be pompous, pretentious, haughty and arrogant, even regarding the people or animals they dedicate themselves to helping.

These kinds of people see human beings as tools just as much as any other narcissist and they will quickly eliminate anyone who tries to come between them and the worship and adoration they feel they deserve.

What can we learn from them?

While we are better off avoiding these kinds of people altogether, there are some valuable lessons we can learn from them. For one thing, their outward confidence makes them almost irresistible to women (as most narcissists are men- but the tables seem to be turning on that fact). Their shallow sense of self-esteem, coupled with the status games they play, makes them seem like paragons of confidence and charisma.

There is also the way they use charm to disarm people around them. One will be surprised by how much a little charm and flattery can grease the wheels in any social situation. Narcissists have this in spades and it is usually the opening move of many of their manipulations with new targets. People are a very important part of the narcissist's game and that can be a useful fact to remember. It's not about you. Make it about your target and you will have them slipping into your hands even faster.

Psychopaths

What is a psychopath?

Psychopaths are some of the most dangerous

people to walk the face of the earth. Of the three parts of the dark triad, they are easily at the top of the list for who to look out for, especially if you yourself are not one. However, the first interesting thing to note is that while all psychopaths are narcissistic, narcissists are not necessarily going to be psychopathic. Knowing this may be one of the weaknesses that may allow you to spot a psychopath if you find yourself crossing paths with one.

Psychopathy is identified as Antisocial Personality Disorder (APD). It has a lot of characteristics that, similar to narcissism, tend to be misconstrued by the public. This is often due to ignorance or misinformation, like that of the psychotic serial killer one sees in Hollywood movies. While this image isn't entirely untrue, largely due to the fact that these people are the most likely within the dark triad to become abusers and serial killers, many psychopaths are actually very good at blending into society. In fact, psychopaths are often well educated and intelligent.

Regardless of how well they blend into society, there is a way to help unearth the truth about them. Firstly, they will often have the same grandiose sense of self mixed in with compulsive lying and highly manipulative behavior that shows no regard for morality or the wellbeing of others. For one thing, research shows that they tend to be born the way they are. This means that your average psychopath, educated or not, will probably show a history of bad behavior from an early age. They may even have a criminal record.

Brain scans carried out on psychopaths show that the parts of the brain that are activated when most people feel stress, guilt, or empathy remain inactive when they are given stimuli that are meant to trigger these kinds of feelings(MedCircle, 2018). Their very autonomic system (which is largely responsible for reflective responses like the fight or flight and the immune system etc.) are wired differently from most peoples. This is a huge part of the reason that, depending on the kind of psychopath, you will find that they often excel and be found in higher concentrations in occupations such as lawyers, stockbrokers, assassins, salespeople, surgeons and (quite surprisingly) chefs.

What how do they operate?

High functioning- while people think that the term psychopathy is monolithic, it actually has two subcategories that are important to understand if one is to know what to look out for. The first of these being the high functioning psychopath.

These people are just more controlled and calculating. They are far less likely to become serial killers and rather channel that energy into something else, like their careers. In fact, these kinds of psychopaths are far more likely to be seen occupying high power jobs like CEOs of companies.

Don't think this makes them anything like the rest of society. These people are still vicious predators who will eliminate anyone in their way with a ruthlessness most people are not capable of. They aren't afraid to go as far as commit murder or ruin a business at the cost of countless people losing their livelihoods. They are incapable of remorse or shame and will not lose any sleep over their actions.

Low functioning- these are more the types we see in the slasher movies in theatres. The low functioning psychopath usually has a much more difficult time managing their instincts and emotions, so they are far more likely to become serial killers. However, they just don't operate the way most people would imagine.

They are more likely to draw their victims in with charm, or glibness. This is when they prepare to ruin their target's life. They are still calculating, but don't have the ability to redirect those instincts the way their high functioning counterparts do.

They still tend to be very good at concealing their true selves under a veil of normalcy. They are great liars, so leading a double life is not difficult for them. They are typically also well educated, so hiding their actions is no great feat since psychopaths generally seem to be intelligent people. So don't count on them giving themselves away so easily.

What can we learn from them?

Now as dangerous as the psychopath might be, regardless of their specific brand of crazy, they are not to be ignored. They have a lot to teach, especially for those who are looking for upward mobility in life. These skilled predators among us are good to study for multiple reasons, the most obvious one probably being one's own safety.

While they only make up about 1% of any given population, you will find that it still makes a lot of people when you consider how many people there are on planet earth. This means that there is a very good chance that everyone will meet at least one psychopath in their life. So it probably for the best that you know how to identify them and act accordingly for your own best interest and for that of those close to you.

One of the best things we can learn from psychopaths is their ability to detach their emotions from any action. While this cannot be mastered to the same degree by most people, it can be adopted to a certain extent. Finding detachment from the things and people around us can be a great end in itself, but it can also be a great starting point for transforming one's life. One does not need to become cold to everything and everyone they know and love. It is good enough that one simply learn to embrace solitude so that they can focus more on their own self-interest.

Another thing that we can learn from these people is how to remain calm. This becomes especially important during times of crisis.

Psychopaths are not easily affected by stress. This gives them the ability to calmly assess any given situation and act accordingly. What's more, they are not as likely to suffer from paralysis by analysis. Their autonomic systems are a big part of the reason they are so unmoved by taking risks.

Chapter 4: How to read & manipulate people

Reading People

Why learn to read people?

One would be surprised at how much easier it becomes to manipulate people when you know how to read their nonverbal communication. If information is king in the game of manipulation, then reading people is the queen as it allows you to almost see their thoughts.

Body language

Proximity-Proximity is one of the easiest ways to see how people feel about you or other people. Depending on the person's culture, you can often see how comfortable or intimate someone is around you or other people by looking at how close they stand or sit to them. The less comfortable they are, the greater the distance they're likely to put between themselves and others.

Posture:

Head posture- the way someone moves or holds their heads can tell you a lot about where they are in their own head. Watching where they point their chin can tell you if they are confident, the chin will be up; aggressive, the chin will be up and pointed forward; or insecure or sad, the chin will probably facing down.

Open posture- a good way of seeing if someone is warming up to you or someone else is to see if their body is open and relaxed, usually exposing their chest. This is most common in men. Women will sometimes lean in and point their body towards you to show interest in you or what you're saying.

Closed posture- this is a good way of telling if someone is uninterested in or unsure of a certain place or interaction. They will usually hunch more as if preparing to fall asleep or duck if the situation calls for it.

Arms and legs:

Hand positions- where people place their hands says a lot about what they want. While people are familiar with how to read touching of other parties, they seldom realize how the movements and positions of the hands can be a form of sub-communication as well.

Unconscious pointing- some people, depending on how gestures are viewed in their culture, are likely to point their hands or fingers in the direction they may want to go without realizing it.

Concealed hands- someone trying to hide their hands by folding them, putting them in their pockets or behind their backs can often show defensiveness or deceptiveness. They are instinctively trying to hide a part of themselves.

Holding the head up- people using one hand to hold their head up is normally a sign that they are paying attention the best they can. Holding their heads up with both hands is more likely to mean they are bored and ready to leave or fall asleep.

Creating barrier- people keeping their arms or some object they're holding in front of them can often mean they are using it as a barrier between themselves and whoever they're interacting with. This can usually show disinterest, boredom or uncertainty.

Crossing arms- this is not always to be seen as a sign of disinterest or even negative emotion. In a lot of cases, confident people will cross their arms when they are feeling comfortable or in charge. So this one must be read with the context in mind.

Hands on hips- this is one of those positions that require context to understand. While this gesture can often be seen as a show of anger, it can also show confidence, depending on where the person is from and their culture.

Feet pointing- the feet can often give some people's intentions away as they are the easiest things to forget during an interaction since they are the farthest body part from the brain. Peoples' feet are most likely to point where the person actually wants to be.

Legs crossed- depending on where the person grew up, the way they cross their legs can usually tell you how comfortable they are depending on whether their legs cross and lean towards or away from the person they are interacting with.

Facial expressions

Happiness- this will usually come in the form of a smile where the lips pull back and up. Their cheeks will usually lift and crow's feet will form around their eyes. Only around one in ten people can fake the crow's feet around the eyes.

Sadness- the inner corners of the eyebrows will usually draw together and up while the mouth pouts and lips turn down at the corners. The jaw will usually come forward. This is considered one of the most difficult faces to fake.

Surprise- the eyebrows will rise, stretching the skin beneath them while wrinkling the skin above them. The jaw will usually loosen or drop while the eyes will open up wider, making the whites of the eyes more visible.

Fear- similar to when surprised, the eyebrows will rise, but this time in a straight line rather than a curved one and the wrinkles will be closer to the center of than across the forehead. The upper whites of the eyes usually show while the jaw loosens to scream (flight) or breathe (fight).

Anger- the lower jaw comes forward and the eyebrows are drawn together and down forming vertical wrinkles between the eyebrows. The lips will tighten or form a square depending on what the person.

Disgust- the upper lip will usually be raised, along with the lower lip. The nose will also wrinkle and the cheeks will rise up. Lines will form below the lower eyelid. This is the face most people make when smelling something bad.

Contempt-this is the easiest one to spot as one side of the mouth will rise, creating a sort of smirk. The rest of the face will often remain relaxed.

Understanding the face:

Reading the eyes;

Power gaze- this happens during social interactions, like interviews, where one person (usually in the power position) is assessing the person they're speaking to. This will usually take the form of someone looking back and forth between your eyes and forehead, making a small triangle with their eyes.

Social gaze- this happens between people who know each other well and have a close relationship. They will look from eye to eye, then the lips. However, their eyes may occasionally dart across other parts of the face, but the triangle will still appear.

Intimate gaze- this happens between two people who are very close or have just had an encounter that made them feel extremely close. The eyes will dart back and forth between the eyes and then down at the chest, not necessarily the breast, although that does also happen.

Blinking- this can be a sign of nerves, and potentially deception, if it happens in with a higher than normal frequency. Reduced blinking may also be a sign that someone is aware of their blinking and are trying to control it.

Pupils- the pupils are a great way to see what, or who, someone may want since the pupils tend to dilate when we look at something we want. This happens so that the eye can take in more light and see better.

Eye blocking- this is usually a sign that someone is uninterested or unimpressed and simply doesn't want to keep looking at someone or something. Seeing someone rubbing their eyes hiding them while you're talking is usually not a good sign.

Mouth;

Pursed lips- this can point to someone feeling distaste, distrust or disapproval during a certain interaction. This can happen for less than a second, but can be useful to remember for reading some people.

Lip biting- this is normally a sign that someone is nervous, stressed or anxious. Another time someone may do this is if they are aroused.

Movement

Mirroring- this is a good way to see if someone is fully engaged in an interaction or not. Mirroring usually happens when we are around people we admire, trust or like. Consider changing your posture or using a certain small action, like slightly shifting your weight, to see if someone copies you.

Head nodding- people can nod fast when they are patiently listening to someone. However, fast nodding is usually a sign that someone is eager to start talking themselves or simply leave as fast as they can.

Head shaking- shaking the head side-to-side can happen when people disagree or are in disbelief of something. This is said to be one of those expressions that formed by how we learn to refuse food we as infants.

Head tilting- someone tilting their head to the side is often done when someone is listening intently. Tilting the head back, however, can be a sign of suspicion or uncertainty.

Final tips

Intuition- this can be a great tool for learning how to read people. We won't always have time to think, but our 'gut feeling' will often fill in the blanks. Many people have reported feeling "uneasy" being around a psychopath for the first time despite not knowing who or what they were.

Gauging personality- people who are more introverted will take longer to answer questions as they take time to get their thoughts in order. Extroverts, on the other hand, will answer almost immediately, as if speaking helps them think.

Observe shoes- peoples' shoes tell the story of where they are in life. They also tell us a bit about how they live and perceive themselves or the world around them.

Create a baseline- reading people you just met can be difficult since there are always exceptions to the rules. One of the best ways to read a stranger is to ask them a series of questions they would have no reason to lie about and pay attention as they do.

Look for deviations- when you are more or less familiar with someone's habits, you stand a far better chance of knowing how to read them. This works especially well if you want to spot deception.

Note gesture clusters- it is easier to read someone if you take in their gestures in chunks rather than looking for one or two to give them away. Multiple gestures telling a similar story are far more trustworthy than one.

Split the difference- when you spot contradictory gestures and/or facial expressions, then it's usually a safe bet to pay close attention to the negative ones. So if someone is smiling with their mouth, but not their eyes, that is usually a sign that the smile is fake.

Identify the voice- some people have strong voices while others have weak voices. This does not mean loud voices. There's a difference. People with strong voices are usually more confident and are more likely to be the strongest personality in the room.

Look at the walk- the way people walk can tell a lot about how they are feeling or how they view themselves. People with a more fluid walk or good posture are more likely to have more confidence in themselves.

Listen for operative words- the action words (verbs) people use will often let you know what part of the sentence to pay the most attention to and also what kind of person they probably are. These operative words will usually help one read between the lines.

How to manipulate people

Now that you have learned all the different ways most people will use to manipulate you and how to defend against them, it is finally time that you learn some ways to set up some countermeasures. It is important that you learn this language of manipulation to use it yourself or at least better defend against those who would use it against you in amoral ways.

Whether it is to defend or attack, you want to be well versed in these tools moving forward because you will find your everyday life is full of them. Pay close attention and see the dark side of manipulation continue to unfold before you.

Draw triangles with your eyes

This simple trick, which you will remember from the portion about body language, is a simple trick that most people will not notice even if it was used on them a hundred times. It plays on the mind's subconscious and makes them react instinctively thinking they are making choices themselves.

You simply draw a triangle with your eyes on the other person's face. You start with one eye and then move to another eye. The triangle ends at the forehead. Repeat this enough times and you will find yourself ending an unpleasant conversation much quicker than the other person may have intended. It's great for getting away from people you no longer want to engage without slighting them.

Concession

This is one of the oldest tricks in manipulation. It is so simple and so old that most people figure it out as children, even if they do forget it as adults. This is a simple form of de-escalation to get what you want.

All you need to do is ask for something more outrageous than what you want. When the person you are asking says no, ask them for something smaller. Do this once or twice more until you finally ask them for whatever it was that you originally wanted. After considering the other options, the person you're trying to persuade will be far more likely to say yes.

Slight nodding

Using nodding plays on most people's tendency to mimic people they are watching. It works even better if the person you're using this trick on likes you in some way or the other, but it can also help break down someone who doesn't.

You simply nod slightly as you ask someone for something and they will be more likely to say yes to you. The trick is to make the nod subtle enough that they barely notice it. This will register in the subconscious part of the mind and bypass the logical parts of the mind altogether.

If nothing else, learn to notice how often people are inclined to agree with people who use this technique or even how much more you're likely to want to say yes when you see it used on you.

Align with opposition

If you know that someone is planning on attacking your conduct or performance at a meeting or something, then the best thing to do is avoid the instinct to create distance between you and them. In fact, you want to sit as close to your opponent as you possibly can. The best place to sit is right next to them.

This will reduce the likelihood of them singling you out the way they intended because you are sitting so close; it makes the mind think you are on their side since you are both facing the same direction. It is a subtle deception, but a good one to know if you are to avoid public embarrassment.

Use because

This one is fairly new to the world of manipulation, but has been proven time and time again to work. Studies have shown that people who use the word 'because' to explain the reasoning behind why they should get what they want will receive it a lot more often than people who don't use it. The funny thing about this technique is that the reason didn't even have to be a good one. They were still more likely to get what they wanted if the justification was weak.

This will not guarantee that one gets what they want every time. It simply increases the chances that their request is fulfilled.

Mimic body language

Another easy-to-use tactic is copying your opponent's body language in subtle ways. It works well because people are more likely to build a rapport with people they feel they have something in common with. When they see you showing some of their own mannerisms to them, then they will think you are more like them and be more inclined to listen to you.

Simply observe someone's body language and subtly copy some gesture or posture of theirs, like how they stand. This will make them want to like you more, which is the cornerstone of many a covert manipulation technique. Once they like you, then you are far more likely to successfully conceal your manipulations.

Ask favors

If you ever want to get someone to see you in a different light, then ask them to do you a small favor that is well within their power. This will work even better if the favor has nothing to do with work or any other serious context. The more social and seemingly detached then the better.

This will make people want to change their perspective of you, even if they don't like you. Having the feeling that they can positively contribute to your life, making you a little more 'reliant' on them, then the more they will want to see you as a possible ally. It can be as simple as asking the target to lend you a book.

Reciprocity

Asking favors is very similar to creating a need for your opponent to reciprocate. It does not have to be in a big way. Just find some small way you can do something that your target will consider a favor and they will feel the need to return that favor in some way. It does not have to be a big favor that forces you to go out of your way at all. They might see that as threatening or consider you someone they can exploit. Simply find some small thing you can do for them and they will consider you someone they like and become more open to doing as you please.

Use silence

Silence is one of the most underrated ways of getting information out of people. Most people do not appreciate drawn out silences in the middle of conversations. They will usually try pretty hard to fill these dead spaces with more words and divulge things they may not have meant to.

All you have to do is ask someone a question and then maintain eye contact even if they break it. Say nothing after they stop talking and just keep looking at them. This will make them so uncomfortable that they will want to fill the silence and put you at ease. This is usually when they will start saying whatever else it was they were trying to hide.

Use pauses

Pauses are also an underutilized tool when it comes to secretly controlling people during conversations. It is simple and far less uncomfortable than longer silences that are drawn out while adding more gravity to the point you were trying to make.

Next time you are about to say something important, slow down and take a small pause before making the point or saying a certain word you wanted to say. The pause creates some tension that your continued speech will relieve and the words that follow it will seem to carry more depth than they would have without it. This will instantly make any argument seem stronger.

Persistence

One would be surprised by how much they lose out on just because they gave up on a request a bit too soon. People are often more compliant than one realizes, and it doesn't take much to break through the initial barrier they put up.

Persistence does not have to be obnoxious. It can be as easy as keeping the conversation going a few more moments before asking again after a minute or two. It helps if the same question can be presented in a slightly different way each time. People will sometimes relent as soon as the second or third attempt, so never take an initial 'no' at face-value.

Social proof

Social proof is the simple act of using public approval in your favor. The more other people speak well of you or something you try to put across then the more likely it is that the people you want to convince will take the bait.

Humans have evolved to be social creatures and as such are easier to be influenced by what groups of people do or say in unison. This is doubly true if the group of people relates to us in some way or the other be they or the same gender, culture, religion, sexual orientation etc. Social proof can be done in a number of ways and can be adapted to a specific target, so it's always safe to branch out and get creative, then step back. It can backfire if it is too obviously orchestrated by you, for you.

Create scarcity mindset

A lot of seducers and salespeople will use this tactic, but it can be used in many different kinds of negotiations. Any time there is a chance to get the upper hand in a negotiation then it is vital that one presents the object of the negotiation as rare and difficult to find.

This tactic works because of how well it plays on the mind's fear of loss and its love of novelty at once. This is why finding what makes anything or person seem unique can win over an opponent and make them buy into the persuasion.

Use fear

Fear is one favorite technique that people in power love to use to keep people below them in line. However, this tool is far more versatile than that. It can work even in sales talks or relationships.

Once a certain fear has been established and its fires stoked, then it is important to relieve that fear. Whatever antidote is offered to a fearful mind is far more likely to be accepted. Give someone what they believe is the best, or even the only, remedy to the object of their fear and they are far less likely to disagree or refuse. Persuasion is a game of emotions winning over intellect.

Use authority

Authority is an amazing tool to have in your arsenal when looking to get your way. People are far more likely to submit to someone they consider a senior or superior of some sort. There are a number of ways to increase the illusion of one's authority or diminishing that of another. It simply comes to knowing the tools at your disposal and which will work best on a given target.

If one's own authority is still not enough then conjuring a figure of authority will work just as well, so long as they are on your side. This is why even something as small as stating a fact backed up by some respectable figure can win an argument.

Chapter 5: Dark Seduction

Now there are multiple ways to seduce people. Although there are many different things that will appeal to many different people, there are many basic rules that apply to both genders that one needs to pay attention to in order to successfully seduce someone.

Seduction doesn't have to be about sex. It can be used anywhere as a powerful negotiation tool, since being liked is one of the best ways to get what you want with little to no resistance. This makes seduction a powerful tool to learn how to use against someone or prevent it from being used against you.

Seducing men

Be confident

Confidence is something that appeals to most men because it communicates that they are seeing prey worthy of chasing. The more you see yourself as being worth the chase, then the more they will see you in the same light.

It's more of a certain mindset that seeps into your body language and general way of expressing yourself. Men can spot this from a distance and it drives most crazy. However, inauthentic confidence can wreak of insecurity and desperation.

Confidence needs to subtly express itself from a place of truth and then others will start to recognize it as genuine. Only once it's calibrated to seem as authentic as possible will it sell and start having men look at someone they may not even have considered that physically attractive in the beginning.

Wear flattering clothing

Flattering clothing does not entail showing all the flesh one can without being technically naked. The most flattering clothing is the type that makes men wonder what lies underneath. That is when your clothing becomes the most effective.

Form fitting clothing that creates as much of an hourglass figure as possible will count far more than clothes that make one seem as skinny as possible. Men tend to be more attracted to shapes than sizes. Skinny is not a shape.

Wearing things that occasionally show a bit of something they shouldn't is a great way to seduce men. This works especially well on dates or when going out. Showing up all covered up but with a skirt that shows a lot of your leg when you sit a certain way or walk at a certain speed will have his eyes darting there every second they get a chance.

Eye contact

This is especially difficult for many people to do in regular circumstances. It can feel almost impossible when looking at someone you really want to like you. It becomes harder still when you like them back. This is made even worse when one is lacking in confidence.

Unfortunately, eye contact is important in seduction. Most men will focus a bit more on the eyes when looking for clues that they have a chance. Learning how to communicate your intentions with your eyes is one of the best ways to flirt without having to worry about using words to get the message across.

The easiest way to master this is by looking at your face in the mirror or in video recordings while speaking about things that make you feel a certain way, so you can know what your face probably does when you feel or think about certain things so you can trigger that at will.

Touch

Touch is one of the easiest things to get wrong when seducing men. While touch doesn't always say that you may be attracted to them, it is common knowledge these days that it can be a good indicator of attraction. If used carelessly, it can seem desperate.

The most well-known and obvious ways are to use touch to direct it towards a body part that the man might be proud of, like his bulging biceps. There's a good chance that area gets attention all the time and your touch will hardly stick out.

Something most would not think to complement and then touch that in a playful way. Perhaps run your touch along his skinny shoulder or run your fingers down his fleshy chest and watch his face light up as he suddenly feels like you see him in a way no one else does.

Play hot and cold

The last thing anyone wants, male or female, is to look desperate when trying to seduce someone. Men are notorious for avoiding women who show even the slightest signs of desperation. Going hot and cold can be a great way to avoid falling into this trap.

Once an attraction has been established and a little flirting has been done, it is safe to let him sweat a little. It doesn't have to be drastic. It can be as simple as suddenly having to go catch up with a friend for a few minutes or even allowing a little boredom to show mid-conversation.

Anything that momentarily changes the energy will play to your advantage. Once he has to wait for you a bit or work a little harder to keep the conversation going then he will feel the chase is worth his while.

Use silences

It makes sense to want to squash all silences that might occur in a flirtatious exchange. It's purely natural as they may be a signal of a lit fire cooling down. However, this is a mistake.

Silences can be a great way to increase sexual tension by letting them build. One can choose to punctuate them with a playful touch or a moment of prolonged eye contact. These are can lead up to what Hollywood has dubbed 'moments'. They don't have to be accidents like what we see in the movies. They can be as calculated as a good outfit.

Use awkward situations

People often think that grace and poise are absolutely essential when seducing someone, but this is not always the case. Use what you have to your advantage as if it were on purpose. If you are clumsy, then let him catch you if you accidentally trip. If you lack spatial awareness, then let your leg occasionally brush up against his. These kinds of moments will often set the heads and hearts of most men racing.

These kinds of occurrences are very risky though and are best exploited when they occur naturally. Being caught trying to create one of these moments can send a man running in the wrong direction. They are best suited for the genuinely awkward or the skilled thespian.

Flirt

There is nothing more confusing than having a conversation go well just to end up being seen as a friend or less. If seduction is the goal, then the conversation has to, at some point, take on some sexual undertones. These are to establish that sex is on the table without ever saying it out loud.

Flirting can come in many forms and needs to be calibrated to the situation, but it all eventually boils down to the same thing. Sex. Or at least the possibility of it. Creating, in his mind, the idea that sex might happen without actually saying it or even hinting at it too strongly will keep him wanting to play as long as you need him to. The best way to do this is to have conversations that might revolve around sex while having little to nothing to do with it.

Smile

Smiling at a man can go a long way. Giving a man a genuine smile can drag him across the room just to talk to you. The key-word is **genuine**. A fake smile can end the game before it even begins.

It is wise to know the different kinds of smiles so as to learn when and how to use them. Know what different kinds of smiles you have and learn when to use them instead of words to increase sexual tension. Look in the mirror and smile for different reasons and see how the smiles themselves change when you feel or think certain things.

A smile can also help ease some of that awkwardness that can build when eye contact is too prolonged or an awkward silence last a little too long.

Share personal information

One of the best ways to get someone to want to be open with you is making them think you trust them. If you can show a little vulnerability here and then while allowing it to be shown as well without showing judgment, unless the target is a masochist, then it will create an air of trust that will make him see you in the right light.

Most men like to have some degree of power, so making him feel like he has your trust will give him a sense of having a little power over you. This act of relinquishing a bit of power can increase the intimacy between two people without them ever having to touch.

Get him alone

One of the most important parts of most seductions will be getting the target alone. Depending on your intentions with them, you want to have them in a space where you can allow your plans to unfold in a timely manner without the target getting distracted. In this space, they are far more open to your influence.

The very act of being alone with someone as a subtle sense of intimacy itself, so at this point it becomes a lot easier to set the right mood for the seduction to be complete. This can be done by challenging him to a game of pool or asking for some company on a cigarette break, etc. It doesn't have to be romantic. It simply has to allow you to isolate the target.

How to seduce women

Choose the right target

There is nothing more depressing than watching someone with a lot of potential wasting it on the wrong prey. Even predators in the wild know to hunt the prey that they're most likely to catch. That is not to say one should lower their standards. In fact, quite the opposite.

One's chances of successfully seducing someone increase substantially when they are looking in an area where they feel most comfortable. Go to events that revolve around your interests and start looking to seduce there. Simply being in a demographic that is more closely aligned with your interests ups your chances to get a suitable mate more than you can imagine. Being in these areas will give a novice seducer a much-needed confidence boost.

Have a passion or mastered skill

There are few things that send women running quicker than an untalented person who seems to have absolutely no drive or ambition. In fact, that will often chase away most people worth being around.

Even if you have no money to woo a woman, having something that shows that you have potential can still play in your favor. Having some skill you mastered or some hobby you are passionate about can be what helps to tip the scales in your favor in two ways.

One: talking passionately about something lights an alluring energy in most men that women find desirable due to what may happen if said energy was to be directed at them.

Two: having something that makes you seem like an expert in a certain field can increase your value in her eyes since she now has a chance to experience a whole new world with you.

Approach indirectly, but quickly

Although patience is ultimately the key when seducing, it is important not to become paralyzed by analysis. Looking at her all night from across the room often won't bring her to you even if she keeps smiling at you.

Make it a point to approach a target within seconds of seeing a target. Once you have open, preferably in a non-sexual way, then you can take your time with the seduction and let things unfold at a relaxed pace.

The intentions of the seducer has to be established fairly early, but that doesn't mean the entire seduction has to be rushed. Find subtle and indirect ways to keep making your intentions known throughout the conversation, but don't be too eager to close or you may give the game away.

Look and smell good

Seduction is an assault on the senses and the emotions. If you can look clean, comfortable and well-groomed then you've already set a strong foundation. Couple that with a good cologne and you are doing a lot of the necessary work before you even open your mouth, especially since women tend to have a stronger sense of smell than men.

Looking good does not imply wearing a suit if you're more of a casual laid back guy. Well-kept sneakers and matching clothes that fit properly are a good start. It's about looking like the most polished version of your current or favorite self. 'Polished authenticity', for lack of a better phrase, is what you're going for.

Pay attention

Everyone has a need. If you can identify a person's needs and see which ones you can fulfil, then you are already on the fast track. This can take a little time and energy, but it will be well worth it. The how is simple to understand and surprisingly easy to execute once you get used to doing it.

The first step is to pay attention. Stop listening to all the voices in your head and use your eyes and ears to read body language and listen to what she's saying. She may be under the impression that you're treating her like the only girl in the world, but you're collecting information on your target.

The next step is to start molding your seduction to the clues she's been giving you from the moment she noticed you exist.

Be confident

Confidence is essential to any seduction. Even insecure seducers who still do well only get the results they do because they have learned to mask their insecurities or use them in ways that make them seem endearing or confident.

The way you carry yourself will say a lot about you and start her forming opinions before you've had a chance to talk. This means you need to be relaxed and confident. Walk around the room like you know that nothing can hurt you and she will be more relaxed in your presence and adopt your energy.

Body language and positive thoughts are usually the best way to go about this. Start talking to yourself in a positive way and it will show in your body. Also, adopting positive gestures and body language can actually trick your mind into being a bit more confident.

Have a sense of humor

Laughter is one of the best ways to drop a women's guard without having to rely on getting her intoxicated. She may regret being with you because she drank too much, but she won't regret being with you because you make her laugh.

It's not about telling jokes or making light of everything. Different things make different people laugh, but one of the most disarming ways most people can adapt to is finding the humor and absurdity in your own life and telling funny stories about that.

Being vulnerable and positive about things that can be seen as negative will make you seem upbeat and possessing a strength of character that she will probably find refreshing.

State your intention

A lot of guys will often feel that they did everything right just to end up losing her interest or ending up in the dreaded 'friend-zone'. This often happens because there was no intention stated early on in the exchange.

Now, this does not imply telling her that you like her straight away and giving away your power. It simply means keeping the conversation around or continuously coming back to naughty, playful topics that somehow revolve around sex.

Having the conversation constantly about, or loosely related to sex will keep the option of sex happening on the table even if it's never stated out loud since saying too much too soon will put too much power in her hands and make her begin to look for more of a challenge.

Isolate her

Make it a point to relocate to a different location as soon as you can. It can be outside the noisy club or from the video game convention to a bar. It doesn't matter. All that counts is that you try to get her to a more intimate setting where you can have her alone.

This makes her far more open to your influence. It is much harder to influence her if she still has her friends around her or you have to keep shouting over loud music. It can be as innocent as claiming that the party seems dead and ask if she wants to go to a bar or something.

Social proof

You will hear a lot of guys in the seduction community talking about proving value. This is a necessary step that can happen in a number of ways, but social proof is probably one of the most effective ways of showing value.

In this context, showing social proof can be showing evidence that you have other people in your life who crave your time and attention. This is best done if those other people are also women who you may not even be sleeping with since women just love having what other women have or want.

Knowing people who can say good things about your or arriving at a place with good friends you seem to be having fun with is a sure sign that it'll be worth her time to hang out with you since you seem to have other people who seem to enjoy your company as well.

Create an air of mystery

You will often hear people talking about making her see you as some kind of challenge. Creating a sense of mystery around yourself is possibly one of the easier methods to pull off.

Simply keep your answers short where possible and make certain things seem like a secret you're not yet ready to reveal. This will give her a puzzle she feels the need to solve and make her want to spend more time with you even if it means chasing you a little.

This will also be a good way of keeping the conversation on her so that you can keep getting the necessary information out of her. Just remember to give her the odd bit of insight into you so she doesn't feel like you're standoffish or closed off lest she loses interest.

Escalate

This is one of the safest ways to try to get a woman where you want her without giving yourself away. If you're slow and calculated about it, you can become far more efficient at seducing women.

Depending on what you are most comfortable with, find ways to keep escalating the sexual tension one notch at a time. If you're talking about partying, start getting the conversation closer to the topic of sex until it becomes about having sex with each other. If she's okay with you touching her elbow, then see if she's okay with you touching her upper arm and eventually her face.

The trick is to move progressively. If she goes with it, then you may proceed to the next level. Lastly, if she doesn't react to it, then you can escalate a little more.

Push-pull

Too much positive energy can give away too much of your power in the game of seduction and that's the last thing you want. It is far better to calibrate your interaction by often throwing in a playful insult, preferably about something she isn't too sensitive about, and then keep going as normal.

One of the simplest ways to do this is to say something a little insulting right after saying something nice to her. You can also mix it up by saying something non-related after saying something nice to pull away from the tension the compliment just created.

Chapter 6: Hypnosis and NLP

What is hypnosis?

This is just the way that people may use hypnosis to influence people around them without their knowledge. This can be thought of as 'covert hypnosis'. It may not always be as hard to detect and malevolent as most people might think. However, its power and widespread influence should never be underestimated.

This involves avoiding the critical thinking portions of the brain and embedding ideas in the deeper parts of the mind that we don't consciously control. While most people will innocently use a lot of these techniques without realizing it, there are those who know exactly what they are doing and intentionally using them on unsuspecting people.

Who is most likely to use it on you?

We come across covert hypnosis all the time without realizing it. While it can't be used to brainwash and mind-control people the way you see on stage or in the movies, it's still a powerful tool for gaining the compliance of people around you.

One will come across it most often in everyday life when advertisers want to get you to buy something. They want your money, not your consent. To this end, they research ways to get you to comply and give them your money without asking questions.

Other people in power who want unquestioned followers will use these techniques as well, like televangelists and politicians.

Tactics

Dominate the subject's attention

The reason you are most likely to see hypnotism used on you while you watch television or surf the web is because that is when you are fully engrossed in what you are doing and are in an attentive state of mind that leaves you highly suggestible.

When someone has your full attention to the point where time seems to fly and everything else seems to matter a bit less is when they have the most power over you. This is when you're more likely to register the things they say on a deeper level than you usually do, to the point of not thinking critically about what they were saying.

Think of the last time you were enjoying a book or conversation to the point where time flew by you. How much time do you think you spent engaging your critical mind to question what was going on and fact check?

Engage imagination

Taking someone on an imaginative journey to some special place in their minds where they are more likely to feel safe is where they are more likely to be open to influence and suggestion. You'll often find hypnotherapists and other types of hypnotists using a method that applies to this principle.

This is because the imagination is a powerful tool. If you can get someone to picture themselves doing something and not regretting it for any reason, then you open them up to a new world where a new option is open to them. As long as the target feels safe and in control then they won't even realize their imagination is being used against them.

Soft commands

This is a great way to bypass the critical part of the brain that registers things like right and wrong. This is more likely to work because trying to give a hard command like, "you **will** lose weight" is less likely to activate any resistance from the critical part of the brain. You will have better chances with a soft command like, "how jealous will your ex be once you've lost weight?"

The brain often doesn't even register this as a command and will focus on the part it finds the most appealing. Just listen to commands that require you to do something without actually asking your consent about whether you want to do said something. This makes you think the idea was all yours when it was actually placed there by someone else.

Linking presupposition

This one is a bit trickier to pull off than one would expect as it requires more finesse than most people are willing to practice to muster. It involves a lot of different elements and can have a lot of moving parts, but can be useful to learn to spot or even use.

Linking presupposition involves asking someone to do something that seems to line up with what they were going to do anyway. Think of someone suggesting you add some special package on a car you're buying even though you may not need it. Sounds familiar right? That's because it is.

When done right, it can make people take on more than they had initially intended. One simply needs to get someone to imagine that taking that small extra step won't do any harm when they were already headed in that direction anyway.

Reality stacking

You will often find politicians and seducers doing this. It involves getting people emotional about things they agree with and then slotting their own agendas in there as if it was a natural extension of the discussion that was missing until just then.

Once you have someone feeling relaxed in the thought that they understand where you're coming from and then aligning yourself with the ideas they carried all along then they will be more likely to see you or your suggestion linking to their ideas as plausible and maybe even natural. You will often hear advertisers doing something similar, especially when advertising for a pharmaceutical company.

The realities don't actually have to have that strong a link to begin with. Just get people saying 'yes' enough times and they will want to keep saying it because it continues a trend. Trends are easier to follow than they are to break, so they'll likely just keep going with it.

Strongly descriptive language

This isn't inherently bad. It's often used by a lot of people when they are trying to tell a really good story. However, there are those who know that the minds love of descriptive knowledge is the quickest path past their logical brain and right to their emotional brain.

It is common for parents to use this language to explain tricky concepts to children since it is easier to understand. On the other hand, it can also be used by manipulators (like lawyers and dark seducers) to get people to believe them without asking too many questions.

Answering a question or telling a story with as much descriptive language as possible will make someone think that they are being told the truth and want to follow the emotional content of the story more than the intellectual content. This is the power of painting word pictures in people's' minds.

Hidden suggestion

The tactic of hiding a suggestion relies on subtle plays on words that might register as a slip of the tongue or the target simply mishearing what was being said. This is more of a one-on-one trick than anything else and requires you to pay attention in case it isn't as innocent as one may think.

The hidden suggestion involves sliding a suggestion in the place of something that sounds very similar. Almost mumbling words like 'die' in the place of words like 'dine' will slowly ingrain the idea of death in someone's mind. It doesn't have to be the said every time, but enough times that it starts to settle in the victim's mind.

Catching someone doing this will not always be easy as they can turn the tables on you and say that they aren't saying it and you must actually have it on your mind if you keep hearing it.

Tone/language mimicry

A dark hypnotist can, in a one-on-one setting, listen out for some of the words a target uses the most when they are feeling a certain way. They can then use them against them when they are trying to invoke certain emotions to lower their opponent's guard and make them more compliant.

This can also be done with vocal tone. If someone memorizes how your voice changes when you say certain things then they can mimic that tone of voice to make people gradually open up to wanting to listen to them when they say particular things in that specific tone.

The ideas said in those moments will feel more like they come from the mind of the target more than they do from the mouth of the manipulator.

Environmental stimulus

A manipulator can open a target to being more agreeable by making it a point to associate certain places with certain emotions. For example, they can give you a small gift every time you pass a certain place until your mind comes to expect it. Once your mind has linked that place with receiving a gift then you are more likely to take on a receptive attitude when you are near that place.

It can also be used to put things in a certain environment that trigger unpleasant emotions. They may put certain things, like images of snakes, in the background of places they want you to feel fear in. Once they have the feelings triggered, they can use the emotional state they induced to slowly change your perception of certain things.

Engage all the senses

Hypnosis works well when it engages as many senses as possible. Once the mind is too busy being engaged on multiple levels, then it starts to lose the ability to focus on detecting threats. Your full attention needs to be where the hypnotist needs it to be.

So when they use words to engage your senses, then your mind becomes too preoccupied to think too hard on things like right and wrong. The heightened state of awareness pointed in another direction makes it easier to subtly plant ideas into the mind of an unsuspecting target.

It relies on the same fundamental principles that are used in magic tricks, pick-pocketing and even martial arts. It's the old story of the magic trick not being where you're looking.

NLP

NLP, which is short for Neuro-Linguistic Programming, is a practice that studies how people map out the world around them in their minds. It also studies how to read these maps people make in their minds and remap them where and when it is necessary. The people who put these kinds of ideas and techniques together were Richard Bandler and John Grinder back in 1975.

While it may use a lot of techniques found in hypnosis, it is important to note that NLP is not hypnosis. It merely draws on the scientific elements of hypnosis, along with many other practices, in an attempt to create a structured way to gain power over 'the voices on their heads' and change their lives.

NLP is widely used by many professionals in high-pressure jobs as well as life coaches in order to get the best out of one's mind in the least harmful ways possible. Many successful people who have used (or still use) NLP will attest to the power of reprogramming one's thoughts and using the mind as a tool to better oneself. However, NLP can also have a very dark side.

Because of the power of self-awareness can create in one's own mind to control themselves, it can also give dark personalities the power to control others. This becomes possible when you realize that the tactics used in NLP can covertly be used on other people once a person becomes adept enough at using them.

State Calibration

State calibration is when one pays very close attention to the person, or people, they are interacting with. They look for the smallest changes in body language. Being well versed in how to read moods and emotions through facial expressions and body language, a person will use this information to change their own state in a way that keeps the other person under their influence.

This touches on the subject of mirroring and works best while still building rapport and deepening the bond one has with a target. Having enough understanding about how thoughts and feelings affect body language can help a neuro-linguistic programmer who knows what they are doing to keep matching or complimenting a person's moods with their own.

Using state calibration well can be a powerful way to build a deep bond with someone and get them in a more trusting mood. Since most people only partially give their attention to people, a target may register this deep reading as the persuader being interested in them to the point of giving them their full attention. People are more likely to like people they are convinced likes them.

On top of building rapport, knowing how to analyze like this may help better detect how someone feels about you, someone else or even themselves. It can also help tell if someone is being deceitful as the moods of most people will change very slightly when they lie.

Anchoring

This is a technique that draws directly from hypnosis. It involves linking a certain emotion to a specific gesture, pose, motion, object, etc. It can be used on oneself or their opponent. It does not have to be negative, but one will see how it can take on darker tones when used by the wrong person.

Anchoring oneself usually begins by getting into a hypnotic trance (it can be done alone or with the help of a skilled practitioner). Once they are here, the hypnotist will ask them to recall a memory that induced a certain emotional state. Once they are in that state they will try to amplify that emotional state by getting them to recall as many sensory memories as they can. This is when they will help them to tie those feelings to a movement or gesture, etc. That chosen pose or gesture will be their anchor. Once this is complete, a person will be able to feel those emotions again by using that anchor when they need to.

If this calls back memories of Pavlov's experiment with conditioning dogs to certain stimuli, then you will be recalling right. This technique draws directly from the findings in that study, which becomes the reason it can be so dark. In the wrong hands, it can be used to train someone to change their feelings towards certain behaviors and adopt different ones.

Frame Control

This can be a simple to use tool that can be powerful during debates and negotiations. While it may have been touched on in earlier chapters, this will now be when the reader will come to a better understanding of how it works.

Controlling the frame is basically presenting an idea in a certain way. Controlling the frame in a conversation or thought pattern is referred to as reframing. An example of how this works is if someone gives you two choices. They are presenting the frame (the operative ideas) of the conversation. Since they presented it, they control it.

How would one then gain control of the frame? By reframing it. This can take the form of introducing a third option into the conversation (if we to stick to the previous example) that the other person will now have to consider. So the person who presents the frame controls it, but the other one can regain it by reframing it.

Dissociation

This is a visualization technique that can help someone overcome negative emotions during stressful situations. Psychopaths are often successful liars because they naturally disassociate their emotions from their actions, so they can be completely calm while lying, even when they know they've been caught.

Dissociation, for people who aren't that high in dark personality traits, will have to be done consciously as our brain's chemistry might often work against us when we most need it to be calm. A good example of how to practice this is to picture yourself outside of your body when facing a stressful situation. Observe the object of your stress and try switch your roles. Imagine what may be going through the mind of the person you want to seduce, or the boss you're trying to get to like you.

If one wanted to take dissociation a step further, they could turn around and observe themselves. Picture seeing oneself from outside the body and then act as if the body is acting completely separate from the mind and emotions. One can even go as far as to pretend they can control their body remotely while being outside it.

Mapping across

Mapping across is a tactic that falls somewhere between hypnosis and meditation. It can be done to one oneself or another person.

This technique involves using future visualization to make someone more likely to take a certain action in the future under certain circumstances. It involves registering one's emotions about a certain event that will happen in the future and how they will want to react to it. After this, one can then consider how they feel about it deep down at that current point. The last step is to steadily replace the current feelings with the feelings one will want to feel in the possible world of that future even.

So if someone is afraid of something they have to do in the future, they can focus more on how they will feel once that event has taken place and passed. If they keep their focus on the feelings that will come after the event has passed, then their minds will learn to register those feelings rather than the negative ones they may currently feel towards it. By the time the event comes to pass, they will have been programmed (by themselves or others) to feel a certain way about the event which will increase the chances that they will do even better since they won't be going in with negative emotions.

Eliminating bad thoughts

Many people are usually held back from what they want because of negative thoughts that are the result of something that took place sometime in their past and has embedded itself into their subconscious minds.

There are three simple steps one can learn to use to prevent themselves from being overtaken by negative thoughts and act as they want rather than acting as their past dictates they act. The three techniques a person can use to do away with negative thoughts are:

Make bad thoughts intentional

While the natural intuition is to avoid thinking bad thoughts altogether, this may play against someone who is prone to neuroticism and other such negative thoughts.

By actively seeking out the bad thoughts and the memories that may automatically play out in one's head, you train your brain to recognize that you are actually the one who is in control of these thoughts. Over time, you will become desensitized to these negative thoughts. And the feelings attached to them.

Remember thought nature

When you catch yourself distracted by bad thoughts, it may be helpful to pause and observe the thought and its effects on you. When you've identified whether it helps or not, you can tell yourself 'it's just a thought' and dismiss it. Switch your mind to a more helpful or positive thought.

When you keep doing this, you realize that your mind is just a tool that you use and control, not the other way around.

Wash them out

Another method to help rid oneself of negative thoughts is to try to wash them out as they occur. Simply identify a negative thought you want to be free of. Make it as vivid and clear as you possibly can. Once you have, allow the colors to go a dull white and the volume to steadily fade.

Do this with the same thought over and over and you will find that it will become harder and harder to recall it at all.

Chapter 7: Case Studies

While it is important to outline how people who are high in personality traits of the dark triad, it can often feel like something that might never affect us in our daily lives. This feeling can persist regardless of all the examples of everyday situations where people might get caught up in the operations of people with dark personalities.

This can be understood as most of us are inclined to trust those around us and view them the way we want to see them or even as a reflection of how we see ourselves. As such, we will often forgo the objective truth before us and prefer to look at things according to what allows us to put in less effort and reserve some mental energy.

There is no doubt that some people live lives so sterile they believe that they may not ever bump into situations where this knowledge may ever come in handy. Others may just have lives that make them feel like they can do well enough on their own without using these techniques. However, the honest truth is that dark psychology touches all of us daily in an attempt to manipulate us into handing over resources we might otherwise use for our own benefit, like time, money, or even energy.

In light of this, this chapter will highlight a few iconic figures in history and the present. This should allow one to see how these dark personalities may reach into our daily lives and affect us despite how our current reality may seem to us. While they may seem a little extreme, it simply goes to show that these people can occupy any part of society they wish and abuse their powers in whatever ways they choose.

Consider this chapter an extension of the dark triad as it links the people, and their stories, to dark psychology to help you better understand how these techniques can be used in different ways. These case studies will serve as practical examples that people can look at and gain a deeper understanding of how dark psychology can be used by them or others on the road to power or even after attaining power.

One can never know enough, so here are a few examples of people who have used (or still use) dark psychology to change history or some crucial element of society as we know it.

Psychopathy

Ted Bundy

Story

Theodore Robert Bundy, born November 24 in 1946, is one of the world's most notorious serial killers. While many educated professionals struggled to accurately diagnose him, he is still held up as a classic example of a psychopath.

He had a difficult childhood as he did not know his father and spent most of it thinking his mother, with whom he already shared a strained relationship, was his sister. He was raised to believe he was actually adopted by his grandparents since his mother was too ashamed to admit the truth about him being born out of wedlock. Finding out the truth strained the relationship between him and his family further.

He was considered a shy child who seemed normal despite being bullied because he was so quiet while growing up. However, he would mature into a handsome young man who was thought of as being easy to talk to and highly intelligent, even having some normal relationships in university.

While it is not certain exactly how many women he may have killed or assaulted, he has admitted to 28 murders, although he originally denied them for a decade. He even married a woman who believed him innocent until she gave up on him when she found out the truth and ended the marriage.

He often attacked women, who previously let him into their homes, while they slept. He'd beat them nearly to death, or worse, and then desecrate their bodies. Other times he would put his arm in a sling or even just use his conversational skills to get women, who were usually in college, to trust him and get them into a position where they didn't realize how vulnerable they were until it was too late. He would often, depending on his mood, groom and/or decapitate their lifeless bodies before proceeding to perform sexual acts on them.

He would go on to represent himself in court and escape detainment multiple times before being caught and executed on January 24, 1989. The media would, perhaps unintentionally, make a celebrity of him. He'd even go onto blame his many monstrous acts on things such as being possessed and pornography.

Link to dark psychology

As you can tell, Bundy fits the profile of a psychopath in a chilling way. He was the model of what an evil person might look like and how they may go about carrying out such gruesome and inhumane acts.

He was charming, intelligent and seemed to have a very high opinion of himself. He regarded himself so highly that he would often become vengeful if a woman were to reject his advances. He thought he deserved what he wanted from people when he wanted it and went into a rage when he didn't get it.

Many people falsely think they would be able to spot someone like this. They imagine evil always has a face that makes it identifiable. This is far from the truth because Bundy, like many other people on the dark triad, don't usually stick out in any significant way. This is compounded by the fact that they often know what they are or may become, so they learn how to walk among us as if they are ordinary people.

On top of being extremely arrogant, to the point where he felt he didn't need a lawyer to represent him in the trial, he was terribly deceptive. These were the kinds of traits that let him escape custody as many times as he did. It also helped him seduce many of his victims into trusting him enough to let him into their lives while barely knowing him. He even had a large female following that adored him, even while they knew why he was being incarcerated.

Narcissist

Kanye West

Story

Kanye Omari West was born in Atlanta Georgia (June 8, 1977). He was the only child and his parents divorced when he was three years old. He went on to live with his mother who would take him whenever she got an opportunity to work. The pair even spent time in China, where young West would continue his education while his mother worked.

It is said that he showed artistic interest from an early age and was always fully supported by his mother. She kept supported him even when he started creating his own music in high-school, having decided that he wanted to take his passion for making music more seriously.

She would go on to pay for him to spend time in a shabby basement studio, making his music. Although not much came directly from the music he made at that time, it did help him catch the attention of DJ/producer No I.D. The two would go on to have a student/mentor relationship that would greatly impact West and the way he approached making music in the future.

He went onto attend university after graduating high school. He would soon transfer universities and then drop out because he feared that the rigorous schedule would get in the way of his music. While his mother was understandably upset about this, being a university lecturer herself, she would continue to support him as he went on to pursue his music.

West would go into produce hit records for artists like Alicia Keys, Ludacris, and most notably, Jay-Z. It was his mainly his work with Jay-Z that would give him the platform and confidence he needed to begin work on his first album as a rapper.

After surviving a near-fatal car crash, he would go on to release his debut album, 'College Dropout'. The album found critical acclaim and commercial success, which would follow the artist around for the remainder of his career. He would soon go onto become one of the most influential artists of the 20th century and make lasting changes and contributions to hip-hop and pop music.

Link to dark psychology

While anyone calling Kanye West a genius would have a very strong case considering his many achievements in music and other industries like fashion, there are none who seem to call him a genius much more than himself. From the beginning, West has insisted and even demanded that people acknowledge and give him the attention he feels he deserves for his genius even before there was any evidence to back him up.

The only thing that stands out as much as Kanye West's ego, is the controversy it has often sparked. He is prone to offending musicians and fans alike with many of his outlandish stunts and remarks to the point of often alienating and polarizing his own fans. He does all this with what seems like a complete disregard for what anyone will think or feel.

While many might argue that his antics are part of his persona and that it is all just for publicity, one would not struggle to see how he wields the characters of a narcissist to his advantage. It could even be argued that he may be one himself, considering how obsessed he has always been with his outward appearance. It has been one of the highlights of his career. He always makes it a point to be seen in the best light possible, trying to outshine everyone around him.

What sticks out even more is how he constantly manipulates situations and people around him to keep him in the public eye. He courts attention all the time and knows how to push people's buttons to get it. The only person who might be able to beat him at this game is his wife, Kim Kardashian.

Machiavellian

Mao Zedong

Story

Mao Zedong (or Mao Tse-Tung) was an extremely powerful Chinese leader born (December 26, 1893) in the Hunan province of

China. His parents were hardworking farmers who managed to do quite well for themselves farming and selling their goods. They were able to live fairly comfortable lives because of this.

Although he was considered a good student, he was eventually forced to leave school at a young age. The sources differ on why he left, but his father soon put him to work on the fields of his farm to prepare him for manhood. As such he would later try to force him into a marriage as well.

While it is unclear what happened between him and his young wife, Zedong himself seems to say he didn't acknowledge the marriage or consent to it. His wife would die very soon after he had left her. He decided to rather go back to school and try to make his own way in the world.

He would soon come into contact with literature that would inspire him to get more involved in serving his country and joined the army. It wasn't long until he found his time with the army complete and he soon found himself some work as a librarian's assistant which may have been what fed his newfound interest in what was going on with Russia at the time.

It wasn't long after this that he decided to get into politics and begin a career that would kill tens of millions of his people, while still being adored by the Chinese public. He would stay in power up until his death on September 9, 1976, as the catalyst who put China on the road to becoming one of the current world superpowers.

Link to dark psychology

Zedong showed multiple characteristics that suggest that he may have existed in more than one of the three legs of the dark triad. It could be argued, however, that he was one of the cruelest Machiavellians in history.

While it is uncertain whether he actually enjoyed the suffering he inflicted on the Chinese people, he certainly found it necessary. He would do whatever he felt was necessary to maintain his power over the country and see his goals come to fruition. As long as he was getting what he wanted, it didn't matter what he had to do.

One of the most disturbing facts about his rule is how much his people seemed to adore him despite how many had died as a result of his rule. He was the master of using propaganda and scare tactics to keep people in line and brainwashed, worshipping him almost like a god.

Conclusion

While many will assume they know the dark underbelly of humanity, they do not. They only learn what their own lives have conditioned them to see. They see what their individual histories may dictate they see. They often don't realize that they often see what others want them to see.

We all create an illusion about ourselves, our situations, maybe even our realities. We chose to live in them and portray them as true because it can often make life easier to bear. We do the things we do, not intending on hurting anyone around us. In most cases, you will find that there is usually little to no malice in the words of most people in a civilized society. They go about their business doing the best that they can. Unfortunately, not all of humanity operates like this.

There are people in history, and some living among us today, who seemed have had a natural proclivity for doing what seems unnatural. They operate in ways that seem to baffle the minds of the rest of the population. They can even do things that can turn the stomachs of many decent people.

In order to help dispel some of the mysteries behind the ways of these people, you were shown how they can be a part of our everyday lives as lawyers, leaders, salesmen, public speakers, celebrities, etc. The essence of their very techniques was gutted and presented to you as honestly as possible.

On top of everything you had already learned about dark psychology, you were shown some of the other tactics dark persuaders may use against you in some unexpected settings. This all happened while a clear division between people who use this on purpose and by mistake was maintained as to avoid creating unnecessary suspicion and paranoia, especially in more sensitive readers. The journey would only get darker from there.

While you dove into the personality traits of these kinds of people, you were given a lot of insight into what makes people who can be considered as having 'dark personalities' tick. Hopefully, you have gained valuable knowledge regarding how these people may operate. Perhaps you even learned about the best ways to adopt some of these stratagems for your own benefit. How you use them is completely up to you.

One of the greatest tools in changing your own life for the better is learning to read people. Knowing the way other people communicate is a great way to improve one's own communication skills without saying a word. That is why it was imperative that you learn how you can read others because others are always reading you.

Manipulation was a necessary evil to learn about as it exists all around us. Learning about this was a natural extension of learning about reading people as the two go hand-in-hand. This is especially true because of all the things you may have found in this book, reading and manipulation are the only two everyone does as reflexively as they draw breath. There is no end to telling how vital this information can be if taken seriously, especially for those who want to have more of a say in the partners they end up with.

Seduction has so much information surrounding it that it could have become its own book. There is no end to the number of people who would like to change their luck with love. While there are many different ways to seduce people, especially depending on whether they are male or female, it is crucial to know that many of the seduction techniques overlap for both genders regardless of their sexuality. Although nuanced differences do exist, it is important to note that when it comes to love, most people want very similar things.

Hypnotism and NLP are techniques most don't know about despite their scientific grounding. There are countless studies that show the power of hypnosis to change peoples' lives for the better. One simply needs to know when they are in the presence of someone that might try to induce hypnosis against their own will. It is widely claimed to be impossible to use hypnosis to make someone do something they normally wouldn't. For the sake of objectivity, that will be left up to you to decide using the information now at your hands.

NLP is a different animal on its own. It has been creatively reinterpreted by many in spite of its roots being in science. Despite this, there is no counting the number of people across different sectors and industries who absolutely swear by it. However, that is not to say that it hasn't been used in dark ways by people who saw the potential benefit of wielding the power to reprogram people around them.

In order to try to give a slightly more rounded and multidimensional perspective of this whole topic, the reader was provided with some case studies to give some real examples of the dark triad at its finest. This was to give a different way of looking at these dark personalities to try to further embed the understanding of some of the forms they may take. It may help some to help strategize against them where necessary or see how we can incorporate some of their weapons onto our own arsenal.

It has been stated repeatedly that there are dark elements to everyone's psychology. There is nothing inherently wrong with this. The problem comes in when we allow people who lean more heavily on these qualities to wreak havoc in our lives. An even bigger problem is when we allow these traits that exist within us all to express themselves when we are unconscious of them. How can one truly be a good person when they don't even realize that their dark side is walking about without their permission and eating away at some aspect of their lives and the innocent people that are involved?

The writer of this book cannot judge how anyone is. One's character is theirs alone to judge. As such, the way the reader of this book interacts with the information they have now acquired is up to them and no one else. Whether this information is used for right or wrong can only be determined by the wielder's discretion.

Bibliography

7 Mind Games Narcissists Play To Manipulate You And How To Use Them In Your Favor. (June 19, 2018). Retrieved from https://www.lifecoachcode.com/2018/06/19/mind-games-narcissists-play-how-to-use-them/

Ahmetkozan. (n.d.). Kanye West. Retrieved from https://www.imdb.com/name/nm1577190/bio

Balbi, L. (May 12, 2014). The Canadian Bar Association. Secrets Revealed: 95 Tips on Becoming a Better Lawyer. Retrieved from https://www.cba.org/Publications-Resources/CBA-Practice-Link/Young-Lawyers/2014/Secrets-Revealed-95-Tips-on-Becoming-a-Better-Lawy

Bandler, R, & Grinder J. (n.d.) The Structure of Magic. Retrieved from https://books.google.co.za/books/about/The_Structure_of_Magic.html?id=sHtHAAAAMAAJ&source=kp_book_description&redir_esc=y

Bariso, J. (November 24, 2015). An FBI Agent Shares 9 Secrets to Reading People. Retrieved from https://www.inc.com/justin-bariso/an-fbi-agents-9-ways-to-read-people.html

BDC. (n.d.). 9 secrets for closing sales with highly informed customers. Retrieved from https://www.bdc.ca/en/articles-tools/marketing-sales-export/sales/pages/how-sell-more-effectively.aspx

Better Public Speaking Becoming a Confident, Compelling Speaker. (n.d.). Retrieved from https://www.mindtools.com/CommSkll/PublicSpeaking.htm

Biography.com editors. (April 17, 2019). Donald Trump. Retrieved from https://www.biography.com/us-president/donald-trump

Bright Side. (January 08, 2019). 10 simple tricks to manipulate people's mind [Video file]. Retrieved from https://www.youtube.com/watch?v=TI2RUxq7N4k

Charisma On Command. (November 05, 2018). 7 Reasons Ben Shapiro Is So Dominant In Debates [Video file]. Retrieved from https://www.youtube.com/watch?v=JY5t6iUzajk

Cherry, K. (April 06, 2019). How to Read Body Language and Facial Expressions. Retrieved from https://www.verywellmind.com/understand-body-language-and-facial-expressions-4147228

Clark, B. (June 09, 2009). Five Ways to Persuade Like a Silver-Tongued Trial Lawyer. Retrieved from https://www.copyblogger.com/persuade-like-a-trial-lawyer/

CloudBiography. (June 14, 2012). Mao Zedong Biography [Video file]. Retrieved from https://www.youtube.com/watch?v=ujbapnrAKXA

Damon Cart. [Life Mastery Gym]. (October 28, 2016). 3 NLP Techniques you must know [Video file]. Retrieved from Life Gym - https://www.youtube.com/watch?v=DhB9fE-TQow

Daskal, L. (November 09, 2016). 21 Ways to Be a Better Leader. Retrieved from https://www.inc.com/lolly-daskal/21-ways-to-be-a-better-leader.html

Davies, J. (January 25, 2019). 8 Brainwashing Techniques Manipulators Use (without You Even Knowing). Retrieved from https://www.learning-mind.com/brainwashing-techniques/

Davis, C. (September 03, 2018). 8 Sales Habits of Highly Effective Sales People. Retrieved from https://www.superoffice.com/blog/8-habits-highly-effective-sales-people/

Depression Alliance. (April 09, 2019). Famous Narcissists: You'll Never Guess #5. Retrieved from https://www.depressionalliance.org/famous-narcissists/

Discover People Skills Strategies Backed by Science. (n.d.). Retrieved from https://www.scienceofpeople.com/microexpressions/..

Edwards, G (April 28, 2016). Top 10 Brainwashing Techniques. Retrieved from https://listverse.com/2016/04/29/top-10-brainwashing-and-mind-control-techniques/

EhowHealth. (April 24, 2009). Hypnotism Facts : how to hypnotize people secretly [Video file]. Retrieved from https://www.youtube.com/watch?v=_qi5LMN4cQc

FarFromAverage. (March 10, 2017). HOW TO

READ ANYONE INSTANTLY [Video file]. Retrieved from https://www.youtube.com/watch?v=LZmPQAc Bspk

Fergus, G. (July 31, 2018). How trial attorneys persuade the jury. Retrieved from https://www.ferguslegalip.com/blog/2018/07/h ow-trial-attorneys-persuade-the-jury.shtml

Goulding, C. (February 04, 2014). 11 Ways To Become The Greatest Public Speaker. Retrieved from https://www.lifehack.org/articles/productivity/ 11-ways-become-the-greatest-public-speaker.html

Hartley, Dale. (n.d). Machiavellians: Self-Made or Born that Way?. Retrieved from https://www.psychologytoday.com/us/blog/ma chiavellians-gulling-the-rubes/201711/machiavellians-self-made-or-born-way

Heryati, R. (January 11, 2019). Qualities That Define a Good Leader (13 Personal Traits). Retrieved from https://inside.6q.io/qualities-that-define-a-good-leader/

How to Read Body Language - Revealing Secrets

Behind Nonverbal Cues. (March 08, 2018). Retrieved from https://fremont.edu/how-to-read-body-language-revealing-the-secrets-behind-common-nonverbal-cues/

Hurst, K. (March 13, 2019). What Is NLP? 5 NLP Techniques That Will Transform Your Life. Retrieved from http://www.thelawofattraction.com/5-nlp-techniques-will-transform-life/

Hypnodoctor. (n.d.). How to Hypnotize People Without Them Knowing. Retrieved from https://hobbylark.com/performing-arts/How-To-Hypnotize-People-Without-Them-Knowing

InsightJunky. (September 17, 2017). HOW TO MANIPULATE PEOPLE(Ethically) - How to influence people by Robert Cialdini [Video file]. Retrieved from https://www.youtube.com/watch?v=F1ZRdsHCodE

Jameson, S. (October 07, 2018). 15 Ways To Seduce A Man & Make Him Crazy For You!. Retrieved from https://badgirlsbible.com/how-to-seduce-a-man

Jenkins, J. (January 20, 2019). Encyclopædia Britannica. Retrieved from https://www.britannica.com/biography/Ted-Bundy

Jenkins, J. (April 08, 2019). Encyclopædia Britannica. Retrieved from https://www.britannica.com/biography/Donald-Trump

Jones, J. (December 21, 2018). Dark Psychology & Manipulation: Are You Unknowingly Using Them?. Retrieved from http://drjasonjones.com/dark_psychology/

Jones, J. (December 22, 2018). How to Connect and Influence with Body Language and Similarity. Retrieved from http://drjasonjones.com/influence/

KamaTV. (August 27, 2017). How to seduce a woman? [Video file]. Retrieved from https://www.youtube.com/watch?v=hvGxYmmDzgU

Kloppers, M. (n.d.). Games and Manipulation: The Games People Play. Retrieved from https://www.mentalhelp.net/blogs/games-and-manipulation-the-games-people-play/

Krantz, R. (April 23, 2018). 15 Sexy Ways To Seduce A Woman That Actually Work. Retrieved from https://thefreshtoast.com/sex/15-ways-seduce-woman-actually-work/

Lao, R. (Dec 22, 2010). Mind Control Brainwashing Techniques [Video File]. Retrieved from https://www.youtube.com/watch?v=J7xi-UJCKF0

Lamb, B. (February 28, 2018). The Story of Kanye West, Controversial Rap Star. Retrieved from https://www.thoughtco.com/kanye-west-biography-3244755

Layton, J. (May 01, 2019). How Brainwashing Works. Retrieved from https://science.howstuffworks.com/life/inside-the-mind/human-brain/brainwashing1.htm

LoDolce, A. (May 25, 2018). How to Seduce a Man: 10 Proven Ways To Make Him Want You Bad. Retrieved from https://sexyconfidence.com/how-to-seduce-a-man/

LovePanky. (July 27, 2017). How to Seduce a Man Who's Not Yet Yours: And Leave Him Smitten!. Retrieved from https://www.lovepanky.com/women/attracting-and-dating-men/how-to-seduce-a-man

Moscovici, C. (August 27, 2015). Dangerous Mind Games: How Psychopaths Manipulate and Deceive. Retrieved from https://psychopathyawareness.wordpress.com/2011/09/13/dangerous-mind-games-how-psychopaths-manipulate-and-deceive/

Murphy, B. (n.d.). 11 Psychological Tricks to Manipulate People, Ranked in Order of Pure Evilness. Retrieved from https://www.inc.com/bill-murphy-jr/evil-psychological-tricks-to-manipulate-people.html

Narcissistic personality disorder. (November 18, 2017). Retrieved from https://www.mayoclinic.org/diseases-conditions/narcissistic-personality-disorder/symptoms-causes/syc-20366662

NLPTimes. (April 11, 2011). NLP Techniques: How to eliminate unwanted thoughts [Video file]. https://www.youtube.com/watch?v=f81dxIXADfc

Nuccitelli, M. (2006). Dark Psychology: Dark Side of Human Consciousness Concept. Retrieved from https://www.ipredator.co/dark-psychology/

O'Nion, M. (July 24, 2017). Techniques Lawyers Use to Persuade Judges and Jurors. Retreived from https://www.mjonions.com/6-techniques-lawyers-use-persuade-judges-jurors/

Pace, M Dark (n.d.). psychology 101 learn the michael pace. Retrieved from https://issuu.com/mohsino/docs/dark_psychol ogy_101__learn_the_-_mi_8d19de2941c9bf

Practical Psychology. (December 02, 2017). MicroExpressions - reading facial expressions are better than reading body language [Video file]. Retrieved from https://www.youtube.com/watch?v=tu1uzG_EB GM

Ramani, D. [MedCircle]. (June 25, 2018). The 4 types of Narcissism you Need to know [Video file]. Retrieved from https://www.youtube.com/watch?v=_uJs0iGQ NoM

Ramani, D. [MedCircle]. (June 25, 2018). Narcissist, Psychopath, or Sociopath: How to spot the differences [Video file]. Retrieved from https://www.youtube.com/watch?v=6dv8zJiggB s

Robins, A, & St.-Aubin, N. (n.d.). What Makes A

Great Leader?. Retrieved from https://www.officevibe.com/employee-engagement-solution/leadership

Rossen, J. (June 25, 2018). 18 Secrets of Criminal Defense Attorneys. Retrieved from http://mentalfloss.com/article/547920/secrets-of-criminal-defense-attorneys

SBK. (December 18, 2018). How to seduce a girl: A Step-By-Step Guide (2019). Retrieved from https://www.seductionbykamal.com/en/seduce-girl/

Schram, S. (March 14, 2019). Mao Zedong. Retrieved from https://www.britannica.com/biography/Mao-Zedong

Spencer, L. (n.d.). 15+ Effective Public Speaking Skills & Techniques to Master. Retrieved from https://business.tutsplus.com/tutorials/effectiv e-public-speaking-skills-techniques--cms-30848

Starr, R. (August 10, 2017). What Makes a Good Salesperson? 25 Qualities to Look For. Retrieved from https://smallbiztrends.com/2017/08/what-makes-a-good-salesperson.html

Steber, C. (May 07, 2019). These Are The Mind Games Sociopaths Play In Everyday Life That You Need To Watch Out For. Retrieved from https://www.bustle.com/p/13-common-mind-games-sociopaths-play-in-everyday-life-to-watch-out-for-2975623

Tardanico, S. (n.d.). Want To Be A Better Public Speaker? Do What The Pros Do. Retrieved from https://www.forbes.com/sites/susantardanico/2012/05/29/want-to-be-a-better-public-speaker-do-what-the-pros-do/#29764d8a1e17

THE 48 LAWS OF POWER. (n.d.). Retrieved from http://www.elffers.com/low/start/index2.html

The Infographics Show. (November 01, 2018). Sociopath vs Psychopath - what's the difference? [Video file]. Retrieved from https://www.youtube.com/watch?v=UAjAMYaiWnI

The Infographics Show. (April 27, 2018). America's most EVIL serial killer - Ted Bundy [Video file]. Retrieved from https://www.youtube.com/watch?

The Infographics Show. (April 03, 2019). Why Mao Zedong Was The Most Brutal Tyrant [Video file]. Retrieved from https://www.youtube.com/watch?v=g_2FZ-V_4zs

Therapy, H. (December 30, 2017). What is Machiavellianism in Psychology?. Retrieved from https://www.harleytherapy.co.uk/counselling/machiavellianism-psychology.htm

Tyre, D. (n.d.). 8 Keys to Successful Selling for the First-Time Sales Rep. Retrieved from https://blog.hubspot.com/sales/keys-to-successful-selling-for-the-first-time-sales-rep

Whitbourn, S. (n.d.). Shedding Light on Psychology's Dark Triad. Retrieved from https://www.psychologytoday.com/intl/blog/fulfillment-any-age/201301/shedding-light-psychology-s-dark-triad

Zeoli, R. (n.d.). Seven Principles of Effective Public Speaking. Retieved from https://www.amanet.org/articles/seven-principles-of-effective-public-speaking/